Letters in Criticism

LETTERS
IN CRITICISM

by

F. R. Leavis

Edited
with an Introduction by
John Tasker

1974

CHATTO & WINDUS

LONDON

PUBLISHED BY
CHATTO & WINDUS LTD
40 WILLIAM IV STREET
LONDON W.C.2
*

CLARKE, IRWIN & CO. LTD
TORONTO

PR29
L4A4
1974

ISBN 0 7011 2056 8

Printed and bound
in Great Britain by
REDWOOD BURN LIMITED
Trowbridge & Esher.

EDITORIAL NOTE

All the titles to the letters, and all the notes with the exception of that to "A Coterie Programme", have been provided by the editor. Acknowledgment is due to the editors of the newspapers and journals concerned for permission to reprint Dr. Leavis's letters, and to Mrs. Valerie Eliot for permission to include a quotation from a letter by T. S. Eliot.

Contents

CONTENTS

INTRODUCTION

This collection of the published letters, on literary and educational topics, of the first critic of our time, is offered to the public in the belief that an intellectual journey such as his, pursued as it has been with a single-minded and almost French intellectual passion, unique in our country, should not remain incompletely recorded, with frustrating gaps and missing links, and that these letters are an essential part of the total record. Though, as the reader will soon appreciate, they compose a substantial body of criticism, they have hitherto been inaccessible save to diligent subscribers to the various journals in which they originally appeared, and there must be very few who can lay claim to have seen all these letters before, or even the greater number of them. Dr Leavis has clearly made it, if not quite a habit, then certainly the rule, to take every opportunity that came along in the give and take, the cut and thrust of critical commerce, by way of demonstrating his conviction that criticism is of its own essence an enterprise of collaboration, corroboration and cooperation – and not forgetting "the creative quarrel". To read the letters through is to realize what "the *common* pursuit of true judgment" means in practice; or, to put it another way, the letters show Dr Leavis practising what he has preached by "the collaborative enterprise". So we see him arguing, illustrating, defending and contesting; he answers critics courteously or sharply as the occasion may require; he routs scoff and he blights jibe; always endeavouring, through the interchange of opinion and interpretation, to create in the reading public a sense of the literary 'object' which will be generally valid; and through variable assessment, correction and criticism, to establish a common standard and value. Because of this, though the letters are occasional and time-tied as letters to the press must inevitably be, and though they were written without any thought to future publication in book form, they have an enduring interest and a persisting importance. In thus using, so consistently and regularly, and over so lengthy a span of time, an ephemeral means for a serious and continuing principle and purpose, Dr Leavis has made a most original contribution to the letter form, and it seemed ridiculous to me that a large body of letters such as these should languish in forgotten pockets of the past and in obscure holes and corners of back numbers, available only to the most resolute of researchers with all the time in

LETTERS IN CRITICISM

the world on their hands.

Although only Dr Leavis's contributions to the discussions and controversies are here reprinted, the letters must clearly be conceived in the mode of a critical dialogue and dialectic, the other answering, opposing, or complementary 'speaker' being not only the particular individual or individuals Dr Leavis is addressing in the letter, but the common reader himself in active partnership. "This is so, isn't it?" Dr Leavis asks, in quest of that measure of agreement without which critical discussion is impossible, and the whole critical process then becomes an attempt to defy the intransigent subjectivity of taste and establish judgements which enjoy general favour. So that an initial word of thanks, and perhaps placation too, is due to those people involved in any way in the writing of these letters, whether directly in having provoked the letter itself, or indirectly in having been introduced into the debate by a third person. Ideally, I would agree, all the documents in the case should be presented to the reader for his consideration, but that, I am afraid, would be intolerably exhausting for him, and not necessarily very rewarding, since most letters to the press are not intended to survive the issue in which they appear, and only those from an unusually fine mind will have permanent value. Mr Priestley, Professor Daiches, Dr Holloway and Lord Annan had their say at the time the relevant letter was first published, or had their opportunity to have their say, and I do not myself think that Dr Leavis has misrepresented them, or been unfair to them and the other correspondents. The reader is provided with the requisite information should he wish to pursue his own researches in past issues of the newspapers and magazines concerned, and he should certainly bear in mind that there were replies to many of these *Letters in Criticism*, and that in the nature of the literary case there can be no last word.

We are told that letter-writing is a dying art, killed by the telephone and the general way we live now. Yet the relatively late branch of letter-writing to be seen every day in the letters to the editors of the national press seems as robust as it ever was, and if these *Letters in Criticism* are anything to go by, no one need fear the demise of this branch of the art in question. Their qualities of character and intelligence should ensure that they outlast their perishable home and occupy the border land where the topical merges into the durable. Like *Scrutiny* itself, the letters are packed with attempts to reassert, amid the very débris of critical standards, their great importance. The letter "In Defence of *Scrutiny*", for instance, is a veritable Epistle to the

10

Philistines; as a propagandist for criticism Leavis seems to me to have no equal. He is a formidable and even dangerous controversialist in this field, and there are not many who have retreated wholly unworsted by a critical encounter with him. Hence is engendered the smarting sense of humiliation and defeat which has produced those numerous complaints of "Dr Leavis's tone". On those critics who do complain of the tone I would press a quotation from Henry James which could well serve as an epigraph to the present work: "I am hideously, corrosively critical," he wrote to A. C. Benson, who was left in no doubt that James meant what he said. We cannot expect criticism where the will to criticise has itself been criticised out of existence. The function of criticism will never be satisfactorily performed at the drawing-room level. And it is obvious that decorum and the "urbane and Oxford-like manner" which George Borrow commends in *Lavengro* would be out of place in the work of a great, unconstitutional questioner of things established such as F. R. Leavis whose life has been spent in pitched battle at the centre of a cyclone, clearing away the accumulated junk and clutter of centuries, and wrecking a thousand vested interests in the process. *Letters in Criticism* deal with many of the literary *causes célèbres* of the century, they contain important texts about the critical debates, the educational disputes and the cultural controversies of the last forty years, as well as providing a history in miniature of the modern movement in criticism and the incredibly bitter Battle of the Books it brought forth. *Some* sharpness and harshness of tone was hardly avoidable in such circumstances, and with such work to do. Some satirical edge and bite was called for.

The more strictly literary-critical letters have played their part, small but real, in the reorientation of taste Leavis has achieved. The three letters defending Lawrence against Middleton Murry are a case in point: the Laurentian advocate insists over and over again that Lawrence's philosophy of life and his vital beliefs and creative ideas, his "Existenz" and his "intelligibilia", give no support to fascism, and that they can no more be divorced from the art through which they were expressed than the soul from the body. The 'message' and the 'art' are an indivisible whole, and it is because of his total command of the art and the medium that Lawrence is able to convey his message and significance. These letters share the same concern as the very interesting reply to Professor Rosamund Tuve on Milton, in which Leavis contends that with Milton too, as with Lawrence, the poet's medium − his Grand Style − cannot be separated from his "Existenz" and his "intelligibilia", and that any view of him which ignored his theological theme and his religious convictions would be seriously incomplete. Milton has been the Great Debate of the century and a specialized battle of the books has raged round his name, so it is appropriate that several letters here should be devoted to the controversial puritan poet; Leavis's method of critical friction and resolution, his "Yes, but. . .", having a specially effective force where opinions diverge as widely as they do in the case of Milton and where there is so little concurrence of judgement. Other letters which belong to the same group − the critical scandals of the century − are "The Right Approach to Shakespeare" which discusses A. C. Bradley's Shakespeare criticism, "A Coterie Programme" which criticises the neo-Bradleyite reimposition of the sixties, and "Professor Roy Fuller on Shelley".

The letters are full of critical stimulus and provocation, all unmistakably F. R. Leavis's, stamped with his critical signature, immediately recognisable as his from the style, tone and content. He could not be anonymous if he tried. The very style of riposte is his and no one else's, idiosyncratic and biting, as when he takes up V. S. Pritchett's little ballistic missile and returns it with interest: "It may not be addressed to the 'classroom' ", he says, "but it has the air of relying confidently on the right response from the 'boys' ".[1] Of G. Wilson Knight he writes: "The extravagantly privileged kind of creative interpretation he claimed the right to practise became very soon the complete and unresisting slave of an inspired private religion − too inspired to cultivate any useful relation with criticism or literature,"[2] and we identify at once Leavis's sardonic brevity, as we do here too: "That few believe they enjoy, few honestly profess to understand, the Cantos doesn't matter; they can be lectured on, researched on, expounded and appreciated − Eliot's authority has availed wonderfully in the establishing of an American classic. . . . We shall do well not to take up that industry in this country."[3] The two letters on *The Princess Casamassima* contain fruitful hints about the novel; and the relative 'placing' of Hawthorne and Melville, and of *Othello* and *Measure for Measure*, give the reader much food for thought. Then there are the statements of what I will call *pure provocation*, such as that Henry

[1] "Mr. Pritchett's Tropes".

[2] "A Coterie Programme".

[3] "Mr Philip Toynbee as Latin Taggist and Critic" and "The Ezra Pound Industry in England".

12

James's "offer to render 'low' speech is as embarrassing as the late T. S. Eliot's," or the startling admission that "I would without hesitation surrender the whole *oeuvre* of Flaubert for *Dombey and Son* or *Little Dorrit*," an admission that makes one want to jump up and cry out, not "Yes, but. . .", but "No!"

Of the other letters there are many on education, particularly higher education, and these complement the well-known books on the subject, *Education and the University, English Literature in Our Time and the University* and, most recently, *Nor Shall My Sword*. Yet the letters must be read for their own sakes; they do not merely repeat or epitomise the contents of the books. The sense of immediate engagement with the issues of the day is much stronger in the letters too; they seem to exemplify a 'direct method' of criticism. The tribute to the college system in "Professor Trevor-Roper Criticises the University Examination System" could be instanced here. Moreover this set of letters does what Dr Leavis tells us he will not do autobiographically: they document the academic scene as it affected the career and prospects of one outstanding don, and in so doing throw a flood of light on the sickness of the universities. A good example of this is the brilliant reply to John Holloway, "A New 'Establishment' in Criticism?", in which, calling himself 'the outsider', he exonerates himself from the preposterous charge (and what charge could be more preposterous?) of being 'establishment'; "Cambridge 'English': Historical Notes and Ironies" is another — a plain, unvarnished catalogue of the facts.

In spite of his disclaimers at some points, Dr Leavis's concern with fundamentals does verge towards a more philosophic statement from time to time. He tells Mr Lerner, for instance, that "it is in creative literature that one finds the challenge to discover what one's real beliefs and values are," while to Professor Tuve he explains that

> a creative work, when it is such as to challenge and engage us to the full, conveys the artist's basic allegiances, his sense of ultimates, his real beliefs, his completest sincerity, his profoundest feeling and thought about man in relation to the universe. When I say that a great work will inevitably have a profound moral significance I am thinking of such a significance as will need to be described as religious, too. (p.67)

The omnipresent concern with fundamentals is a major unifying factor in the letters; it is seen in the many commentaries on the function of criticism, the function of the literary review, the function of the university, the nature and purpose of an educated public, and on the nature of teaching itself (see on this latter "The Misconceptions of Mr Bateson"). His preoccupation with tradition and continuity is intense and well-known (*For Continuity, The Great Tradition* etc.) so that he can justly claim that "I, at least as much as any critic in our time, have stood for 'tradition' and the importance, for life and thought, of having a vital conception, and a robust and subtle sense, answering to that word." In the same letter, "The Radical Wing of Cambridge English", he writes: "How does one get access to the 'historical past'? — that, surely, is the great problem" — a fine specimen of the type of pregnant suggestion in which the letters abound.

No reader of these letters, however partial his sympathies and superficial his reading, will be able to accuse Leavis of playing the Gallio before contemporary problems or of withdrawing to some glamorous past in the face of the great sociological drifts and upheavals of our day. The very opposite is true. He has been no absentee professor or ivory-tower aesthete and has been observed in the fray more often than most. On the mundane plane, when a finger is pointed at him for political quietism he remarks to Professor Ricks that he "signed the Liberal candidate's nomination paper and subscribed to the Liberal election fund." His critique of modern civilization is not that of someone far removed from what he surveys, but of someone in close and everyday touch with it. The critique began with that exquisite sociological primer *Culture and Environment* and was amplified and updated throughout the letters, making this book Dr Leavis's 'notes towards the definition of culture'. He refers, in a characteristic passage, to the progenitor of *Culture and Environment*, Mrs Leavis's *Fiction and the Reading Public*, and says that "among other things it made a pioneering inquiry into the old working-class culture of which the new processes of civilization were eliminating the traces — an inquiry that was greeted with angry contempt by Harold Laski and the left-wing intellectuals of the nineteen-thirties." With "working-class culture" Dr Leavis is pointing to all the motley humours and defining quirks, all the ways and by-ways and customs and traditions and differences of language and dialect and human approach which go to make up the spiritual identity of an area or people or country — the accumulation of centuries.

We have all seen English culture, and not merely working-class culture, steadily destroyed as with each generation, owing to the incessant change of a technologically-directed civilization, the English tradition, and what it means in human terms to be English, grows noticeably weaker. The loss of the cultural heritage, and the leaching

14

and bleaching of life which it causes, and the oppressive and dangerous vacuum which replaces it, is the great burden of Leavis's socio-educational writings. Society, he protests in many places, is a living organism and not a mechanism, and his criticism of the technological age is that it has no use for the organic,[1] no use for the human qualities which cannot be measured and planned, but which can nevertheless be enfeebled and obliterated. In one of the most important letters, "The Organic Community", he talks of "the human impoverishment that may, un-recognised as such, attend automatically on a technological progress towards a civilization of 'more jam' ": a true and necessary diagnosis even if it is not provable, mensurable and amenable to the assumptions of the statistician, and even if it does give the left-wing and its Harold Laskis a fit. For them the cultural loss has been offset, or rather dis-guised, by the very real improvements in material comfort and the elimination of grinding poverty that modern technology has brought off, and it has been very easy for them to pooh-pooh the doubts of those who saw the other face of technology. But even their blindness and blankness has suffered a few shocks of late; the consequences of the cultural disinheritance of the masses are beginning to press for recognition on even their loath attention, and their very optimism is beginning to sound decidedly factitious. In "The Function of the University at the Present Time" Dr Leavis lists some of the morbid disorders of the affluent society, in which life itself sometimes seems at a loose end, "violence, wanton destructiveness, the drug menace, adolescent promiscuity, permissiveness, the enlightened praise of the young for their 'candour' about sex," sicknesses which are created, intensified and spread by the materialistic social and political philosophy of our age — I will not say by its socialism but rather by its Benthamism. In one of the very latest and most topical of the letters, that dealing with Britain's entry into the European Common Market, and the pertinaciously willed drive towards homogeneity it signifies, a genocidal drive which must weaken English culture still further, Dr Leavis says that the columns of *The Times*

> offer us every day the evidence that the civilization that dooms the masses to "jobs" with no human meaning but the pay they bring, "jobs" made sufferable only by the prospect of leisure, is precarious, sick, and far advanced on a path to death. The leisure ("culture") of such a people is provided for by

[1] See "The Compassion of Lord Annan".

commercial interests into whose calculations nothing enters but the profit-motive, or by organizations whose standards have been in essence commercially determined, and, in the process, that widespread creativity which maintains a living culture and with it the significance necessary to human life has been destroyed.

What truer analysis of the plight of civilization, or of the 'England Question' in the seventies, than this, which as time goes on becomes more and more horribly convincing? Indeed I sometimes think, in my dark moments, that Dr Leavis has here written our civilization's epitaph.

It is not only the 'culture' of mass civilization which is under review and attack in these letters; our intellectual culture is also the subject of a searching inquiry and criticism. Why does he forever attack *us*, the critics wail, why attack what is best in our culture – our noble reformers, our noble Intelligentsia, our noble quality newspapers? In one letter there is a reference to "the blankness of the 'intellectual community' " and I have used the phrase as the title of the letter in order to highlight it. It was to the intellectual sickness of our society that Dr Leavis's last book *Nor Shall My Sword* specifically addressed itself, and since several of these *Letters in Criticism* are replies to the correspondence aroused by the component parts of that book as they were separately published, there seems good reason for bringing *Nor Shall My Sword* to bear on a discussion of *Letters in Criticism*. The two books share many of the same preoccupations, have the same cause at heart, and what I have to say about the former book may in some measure illuminate the present one. The major theme of both books is the Preservation of Letters – how to protect and strengthen the country's intellectual culture from the depredations of a technological philistinism, and stem any further decline of an educated public which has "in general surrendered to the climate of the technological age." It is an important contention of his that in resisting "the blind forces Lord Annan so confidently points to,"[1] elites are necessary: "Minorities can matter," he asserts; "A minority can change the spiritual climate" – for good or ill, he might have added, since the harm that an elite can do is as much his theme as the good, and if we consider the influence of one intellectual elite, the Benthamites, on all social classes in

---

[1] "To Reform the Annanite Reformer". The other quotations in this paragraph are from *Nor Shall My Sword* (Chatto, 1972); I reprint here a few paragraphs from my review of the book in *Books and Bookmen*, December, 1972.

Victorian England, so movingly presented in *Hard Times* and *Dombey and Son*, we cannot but conclude, in all good faith, not only that an intellectual community, however numerically insignificant, can enjoy an influence out of all proportion to its size, but also that the influence can be unfortunate, harmful and even malign. In this way Dr Leavis sees one of the threats to high culture coming from within it, as a sort of fifth column, a threat which he styles, with just irony, "the world of enlightenment". This "world of enlightenment", he goes on, "is the great enemy we have to fight, and to go on fighting, in what from our side is the *creative* battle. There is no Stalingrad to be achieved over that enemy, but we can discredit its clichés, disturb its blank incuria, and undermine its assurance – things which most certainly have to be done, and will only be done if the creative purpose in us is strongly and articulately conscious (which is to say, energized by a realization of what's involved)."

But it is "the world of enlightenment", with all its dirty literary politics, which reviews Dr Leavis's books whenever they come out, for the world of enlightenment has a near monopoly of control of the media of communication to the reading public, and the modern writer and reader is virtually at its mercy. The world of enlightenment does not care to be criticised, it is "only human" after all, and through the channels of criticism it takes its revenge. So it is not surprising that Dr Leavis's books have been widely condemned and derided by the reviewing coagulation *when first published*, and have had to make their reputation without its support and outside its mandate. Stung with intense resentment, the world of enlightenment cries out bitterly at Dr Leavis's characterization of it, but can only do so in ways that inexorably corroborate his criticism. To me his criticism is an excellent exemplification of "the function of criticism at the present time" because it provides us with just the commanding voice of protest required to combat this tentacular monopoly of interests. For the power and influence of "the world of enlightenment", of the intellectual publicists and formers of public opinion, have been prodigious in politics, education, religion and the mass media; because of the modern ease of communications an intellectual pocket can now affect, far more quickly and thoroughly than ever Benthamism could, every stratum of society, and in consequence the danger of a social and intellectual autocracy is very real.

How much has our liberal consensus to accept responsibility for, how much is to be laid at its door! It was not for nothing, and nothing

exaggerated, that Malcolm Muggeridge called "the world of enlightenment" a Pack, referring to its atrocious persecution of anyone arrogant
enough to question its assumptions and defy its authority. It was the
testimony of the Pack which smuggled *Lady Chatterley's Lover* into
legality in its original integrity, on the basis that it was an artistic
masterpiece, amid a fanfare of the vulgarest publicity possible, testimony
which has led directly to the ethos of competing pornographies we now
suffer, whether we will or no; an ethos in which the banning of
pornography is equated with political censorship, the equation being
taken for granted with almost infantile stupidity; an ethos in which the
willingness to porn, if I may coin a verb for the nonce, has become an
imperative to any writer who wishes to be heard on the media, and he
who finds himself unpliable by nature goes to the wall; an ethos in
which even *The Guardian*'s once august pages are enlivened by a porny
strip-cartoon to attract young buyers. True, the liberalising of pornography has all been done in the good name of freedom of expression;
at least they say it has; but freedom of expression's good name has
merely been brought into disrepute in consequence of such fearfully
insensitive missionary zeal, as has that of 'liberal' itself – both cases of
wilful verbicide. Yet Dr Leavis insists on a distinction here – the
distinction between pornography, which is just a masturbatory woman-
substitute, and the serious treatment of sexual relations as part of
human relations, the kind of novelistic analysis of sexual relations to
which both Henry James and the Victorian philosopher F. H. Bradley
looked forward. So that if one finds a pornographic civilization of sexual
substitutes abhorrent, it is not because one found the Victorian taboos
attractive, or that one wants them reimposed. Dr Leavis's interesting
autobiographical letter on "The Banning of *Ulysses*" makes that plain.

To "the world of enlightenment" tradition and the past – the
prescription of time and tested experience – goes for nothing and is
replaced by shifting, fashionable theories without solidity or ground;
stupid ridicule is directed on the bourgeois code at every level, especially
on the family, and the disintegration of our culture deliberately fostered
at every step.[1] The taste of the educated public has suffered a progressive levelling-down and loss of confidence, a progressive middle-
browing and low-browing, again often engineered by forces within the
intellectual fraternity. Destructive notions of reform in education –

---

[1] For a useful comment on this see the chapter on Ibsen, "Revolt in the Abstract",
in Bertrand Russell's *Fact and Fiction* (Allen and Unwin).

18

wildly, lunatically idealistic panaceas – have gained a bigoted allegiance among intellectuals, who have scuttled on to uncountable bandwagons in their undignified lust for the sunshine of general approval. Havoc has been made of our educational system at primary, secondary and tertiary level with almost no effective protest offered, with, on the contrary, a thousand intellectual lips paying their service to the new idols of the academy; witness the expansion of the universities, and their transformation into 'mushrooms of mediocrity', the abolition of the grammar schools, and with them of secondary education, and many other such regressive 'reforms', all of which have been hailed by the intellectual community, or powerful and influential pockets of it, as triumphant break-throughs for enlightenment. "Their attitude towards their work of destruction is to be bland and blank" – this is how Dr Leavis sums up the Cantabrigian reformer in "The Transition from Quality to Quantity in Education", but the charge could be reapplied to a very wide academic panorama. The result of it all is that the intellectual community, whose function is to level-up and nourish what so much in our democratic civilization would level-down and eliminate, has forfeited the respect of society at large, has become a focus for general suspicion and derision, its prestige fallen to a very low ebb.

Just how "the world of enlightenment" relates to what is usually called, in shorthand notation, "the Establishment", is not clear in every detail, but that there is a strong connection is certain. The 'culture' propagated and crusaded by the world of enlightenment passes more and more into the hands of the Establishment for safe-keeping and financial backing, as the private patron becomes either obsolete or an anachronism, and the economy of culture collapses. So the culture of enlightenment infiltrates and pervades the Establishment – and is absorbed there. Bertrand Russell may have had some such fear in mind when he wrote, just before he died, in a valuable analect which for some reason went unremarked by any of the numerous reviewers of the *Autobiography*, in whose third volume it appeared, that "cultural matters should be kept free from the Establishment." Yet on the other hand one wonders whether the analect did not get into the *Autobiography* by some oversight or accident, for its home there is decidedly arbitrary, and it is supplied with no descriptive or explanatory suburb. By 'Establishment' was Lord Russell thinking of (i) the British Council, the Arts Council and the other governmental agencies for the diffusion of a bureaucratically elected 'culture', or (ii) the politicians, or (iii) elites from the world of education, journalism and the church, or (iv) top-powered intellectuals vaguely conceived in the aggregate as an Intelligentsia? The choice seems to be embarrassingly large. Dr Leavis, forthright as ever, defines the academic and literary establishments as well as they can be when he says in "A New 'Establishment' in Criticism?": "For the twenty years of its life *Scrutiny* had to contend against the hostility, overt and covert, intense and wholly unscrupulous, of the academic and literary worlds, or of what I think it reasonable to call the Establishment – the people who had the posts, the salaries, the positions of power, and all the means of promoting and thwarting careers and worldly success." But how to keep cultural matters free from the Establishment, or since in these days of the public patron they can hardly be kept free, how at least to protect them from an interference which does not have their true and real interests at heart? What role does the intellectual community as a whole, without which there would be no high culture, have here?

In lands where social and economic conditions allow some margin for cultural activities, and make provision for educational and intellectual pursuits, the *intellectual* gregariousness of man will find its practical answer in an intellectual community. When mature the community will be found stratified into an Intelligentsia of leaders, artists and writers in general, and a higher-level lay-public of readers with intellectual tastes. The Establishment ('posts, salaries, positions of power') will recruit itself from both. The community may be linked by personal ties, as in the metropolitan coteries and university milieux, but otherwise it is the press and the publishing houses which give the community its sense of cohesion, confidence and solidarity, mould its identity, and keep its members in touch intellectually. It is the function of criticism in its broadest conception to keep the intellectual community in being, to maintain and sustain and stimulate its standards, to create from the community a public for the writer, to disseminate among it "the best that is thought and known in our time," and to make individual members aware that, however separated they may be in space and time, there are channels for communication and media for the meeting of minds.

Where there is the strong and entrenched power of an establishment or coterie or elite within the intellectual community – a "world of enlightenment" say, or a "literary world" – an opposition is necessary in the intellectual as in the parliamentary fields, and if the critical energies are accompanied with intelligence and ethical sensibility, the opposition will be forthcoming. Carlyle and Ruskin formed the opposition to the Benthamites in the Victorian age, and the Leavises have in the same way pitted their weight against the technologico-Benthamites of our own. Ideally a plurality of intellectual centres is required,[1] on the analogy of the publishing houses, to fight intellectual monopoly, to counteract onesidedness and lopsidedness, to emphasize truths that are neglected and to criticise those 'popular opinions' which have been taken to heart in the heat, but not the light, of the moment, and with too little consideration and knowledge, and to restore the balance and sanity of reform and change; so that between the Establishment and the rest of the intellectual public friction can work creatively, disagreement be aired to some consequence, and freedom of speech come to mean something positive. In the last letter in this book Dr Leavis discusses the function of the 'little magazine' and says that "real intellectual and cultural life entails the creative play of differences, some of which may find expression as strong disagreements." That seems to me to express the point beautifully.

But this function, of providing a critical opposition to the prevailing consensus and a check to its overweening assurance, has fallen into abeyance with the notable exception of the Leavises, who have suffered near-total ostracism for most of their lives, and partial ostracism even over the last decade: that is the thanks they have received. "They won't let sleeping dogs lie" – such has been the common complaint. There is no plurality of centres; there is only one standard, standardized, doctrinaire, dogmatic 'point of view' – the liberal consensus, which Leavis characterises as *gleichschaltung*.[2] Cultivated opinion, criticism in the widest sense, is failing to provide an adequate critique of the new orthodoxy; it is failing in its function of reforming the reformers and educating the educators; instead of providing a reasoned resistance to the new conformity, it provides it with a crudity of support, with loud noise and padlocked reasoning, and with all the paraphernalia of propaganda. One remarks a growing sameness of taste, a similarity of judgement, and a standardization of opinion as the Intelligentsia is transformed wholesale into a mouthpiece or sounding-board for the established creeds and catechisms, rather than a coolly appraising and correcting force which might temper excess and expose the more flagrant follies. In fact 'Intelligentsia' and 'Establishment' have come to seem synonymous terms in a way which bodes ill for the cultural health of the country.

[1] See "The Priestley Travesty".

[2] In "Professor Trevor-Roper Criticises the University Examination System".

If then the Intelligentsia is failing to provide the Establishment with the essential critical opposition, if the great majority of intellectuals seem to belong to the same intellectual party, and that party the party in office, it is small wonder that the educated public, what used to be called the common reader, should have developed a very indulgent sense of the standards and the kind of guidance the Intelligentsia ought to have and to give; or that the public should tend to degenerate into a passive receptacle for establishment cultural propaganda; or that it is gullible when it should be critical, and says yes when it should say no – that, in short, it should exhibit all the signs and symptoms of intellectual and cultural conditioning:

> It is only in a coherent, educated and influential reading-public, one capable of responding intelligently and making its response felt, that standards are 'there' for the critic to appeal to: only where there is such a public can he invoke them with any effect. A great fact of the literary history of our time is that such a public no longer exists. The fact is manifested in the difficulty of establishing and keeping alive any serious critical organ. It is manifested in the characteristic uncertainty of tone of Auden's verse, which seems to offer itself to a *public* public, and yet confuses that public with the Group, the coterie, from the consciousness of solidarity with which it draws the confidence for its callow sophistication.

("In Defence of *Scrutiny*")

The higher-level reading-public Dr Leavis mentions here has been debilitated by 'this television age', which tempts with a drove of distractions and a multitude of short cuts and beguilingly cheap pleasures; which gives time so largely and in such generous measure only to snatch it away again, that an eternal vigilance is demanded, a conscious determination to husband and put by time for reading and thought, if literature is to receive any attention at all. If not thus consciously prepared for and insisted on, the hours and days rush madly by, time and energy is frittered away, and serious reading goes by the board. The critic himself becomes a mere entertainer, a substitute not only for the personal response of the reader, but often for the reading itself.

The ever-receding frontiers of knowledge, the increasingly labyrinthine specialization of everything, and the astronomical rise in the number of books an educated man is supposed to read and to form an opinion about, but cannot possibly find the time for, are further factors to which the debilitation of the intellectual public can be attributed. It all

22

means that the public has to accept more and more on trust; by an insidious progression educated people come to think less and less, as they read less and less, for themselves, and to live in the expectation of being spoon-fed and thought-fed by a battalion of experts and authorities, of computerial know-alls, and think-tanks with all the answers. A suspension of intellectual habit and a lapse of standards are the involuntary consequence, and a cultural condition formed in which the charlatan and the careerist can make hay in the sun. The second-rate is mistaken for the first-rate, and the first-rate gets harder and harder to come by — as Matthew Arnold predicted.

Indefatiguably in his books and in these letters Dr Leavis contends that society's problems cannot be solved without an educated public, and that an educated public will not be produced out of thin air — it will only come from a conscious working for and towards one at the universities:

> And in fact nothing will be done unless society commits itself to a sustained creative effort of a new kind — the effort to re-establish an educated, well-informed, responsible and influential public — a public that statesmen, administrators, editors and newspaper proprietors can respect and rely on as well as fear. Society's only conceivable organ for such an effort is the university, conceived as a creative centre of civilization.

("The Function of the University at the Present Time")

This comes from a letter replying to a well-known newspaper proprietor, Mr Cecil King, who, in his recently published Diary, after writing off most contemporary politicians as total duds and duffers, suggested that the country might be saved by a business man's government. I think Dr Leavis's remedy will prove to have more efficacious wisdom in it in the long run.

Some idea of the kind of interest the letters have, and of their importance, has now been given. Any blame attaching to the project rests with the editor who has, over the years, pressed the claims of the letters on Dr Leavis; but it is hoped that the reader will concur in judging their publication well justified. For if cultural matters have been protected from the Establishment, if the collapse of standards is halted, and if the liquidation of English culture and the character of the people proves to be not irremeable after all, then I think some credit for it must go to F. R. Leavis's work, and some of *that* credit to these letters.

JOHN TASKER

23

1. Ronald Bottrall's *The Loosening*
To *The Criterion*: April 1932

Sir, — To write expressing personal dissent from a reviewer's judgment
is in general a vain proceeding, and I know that an editor cannot be
expected to let himself be bothered. But I think it is not the usual
egotistic illusion when I say that this is a special case and that I have
very unusually strong reasons for indulging in the vanity. And perhaps
it may not be altogether a vanity, for, if Mr. F.S. Flint reads my letter,
he may, I believe, be led to agree that the list of twenty books of verse
appended to his *Verse Chronicle* in *The Criterion* for January includes
one that might have rewarded his pains. What these pains were I
vividly realise, and my sympathy solicits me to write. If, I ask myself,
I had been in Mr. Flint's place, and had had regarding the twenty
books in front of me the expectations inevitable in anyone intelligently
interested in modern poetry, should I have spotted the one book
worth notice — and that one, moreover, sponsored by a private press?
I have had the advantage of long familiarity with Mr. Bottrall's work
and of having followed his development, and I ask Mr. Flint to pick
up *The Loosening* again, and, with mind and sensibility untired and
undiscouraged by reams of bad and insignificant verse, read "Salute
to them that know", "We are the End", and "Miles Ingloriosus", and
say whether he still thinks the piece from Mr. Aldous Huxley he des-
pairingly quoted is the best verse to be found among the twenty
books.

Mr. Flint will (and how justified by probability!) shrug at this
suggestion, but a critic of his distinction and experience will admit
that there *may* be something in it. He knows also how rare, how very
rare, an intelligent interest in poetry is, and that if a serious new poet
does not get recognition in *The Criterion* his chances of finding a public
are small. There is nowhere else to look to, with any hope, for an intelligent review; indeed, a press that cannot afford to advertize cannot
expect any kind of notice.

It will be plain by now that I think highly of Mr. Bottrall's work. If
I tried to suggest the kind of value I attribute to it the seeming extrava-
gance might prejudice its chance of fair attention. But no one knows
better than Mr. Flint that even a small achievement of significance in
modern English poetry is so rare as to demand critical notice. And I
shall be very surprised if he does not agree that Mr. Bottrall's achievement is a considerable one. It is not for me to offer him a critical

appraisement, though I am very ready to do so.[1]

And you yourself, sir, whose name[2] appears on the title-page of Mr. Ezra Pound's *Selected Poems,* may read this letter with some sympathy if I add that Mr. Bottrall's work appears to me to be the first serious instance of fecundation by that great modern poem, "Hugh Selwyn Mauberley".

You will in any case believe that I am moved only by disinterested concern for Mr. Bottrall's poetry in particular and English poetry in general, and that I have only a disinterested interest in the Minority Press.[3]

I am, sir,

Very sincerely yours,

F. R. LEAVIS

---

[1] Dr. Leavis wrote a critical study of Ronald Bottrall's poetry in *New Bearings in English Poetry* (Chatto and Windus, 1932).

[2] T. S. Eliot.

[3] The publisher of *The Loosening.*

2. A Candid Critic

To *The Spectator*: April 9, 1932

Sir, — When this morning I belatedly (having been away) read in the *Spectator* for March 26th. Mr. Richard Church's review of my *New Bearings in English Poetry*, I had the impulse to write privately to him, expressing my pleasure. For he is the first critic of my book to perceive that it is not my enthusiasm that makes Mr. Ronald Bottrall a remarkable poet. I have for a long while been trying to win recognition for Mr. Bottrall, who has been almost completely ignored; so I am very grateful to Mr. Church. But it occurs to me that, instead of writing to him privately, I might fairly take the opportunity of correcting certain misapprehensions he seems to me to exhibit. That I do so he may take as a compliment: I was prepared for the usual kind of misrepresentation deriving from anti-highbrow animus, and have not been foolish enough to reply; but Mr. Church is (in the old sense) a candid critic.

If, then, he looks at the offending passage again I think he will agree that he does me an injustice in making me call Keats a "vulgarian." To refer, as I do, to the commonplace that Keats was liable to a certain vulgarity is quite another thing. Must I assure Mr. Church that I admire Keats very much? And must I assure him also that I admire Tennyson? And that I have a liking for Matthew Arnold? I suppose that I can't have made plain enough the point of view from which I criticise the Nineteenth Century tradition, and yet certain sympathetic comments of Mr. Church's seem to show that he understood.

And then, what is this "Cambridge School" in which, according to Mr. Church (and so many other critics) I have "served my apprenticeship"? There is Mr. Richards, to whom everyone concerned with literary criticism during the past decade, and especially at Cambridge, has incurred a debt. But I don't think that he or Cambridge would care to be made responsible for my critical methods or my conclusions. I have myself taught English at Cambridge for a number of years, but I never found the least reason to suppose that my methods had any institutional sanction. My critical approach, which (to my gratification) leads Mr. Church to note that I am "preoccupied with technique,' I have always imagined myself (as I hint in my *Prefatory Note*) to derive from Mr. Eliot as much as from anyone.

Let me conclude by repeating that I do sincerely feel obliged to

Mr. Church; adding, if, Sir, you will permit me, that Mr. Bottrall's book of poems is called *The Loosening*, and is published by the Minority Press, Heffer, Cambridge. —

I am, sir,

Very sincerely yours,

F. R. LEAVIS

3. The Tone of Mr Calder Marshall
To *The New Statesman*: June 10, 1933

Sir, — I am not foolish enough to expect sympathetic reviews of my work, or to be surprised when I am grossly misrepresented even (shall I say?) in THE NEW STATESMAN. I should not have thought of writing in protest merely because your reviewer, "dealing" with me in the current issue, represents me as advocating Marxism, "so that a Communist tyranny can impose the reading of *The Calendar* on an unwilling proletariat," and as prescribing the work in question[1] "as an educational text-book." I say I should not have thought it worth protesting, though the latter account appears to be a wanton parody of something on the dust-cover, and the former reverses the anti-Marxism, implicit and explicit, of what I actually wrote. Perhaps the tone of the review would have been enough to advert your readers, even if your reviewer (deprecating "humourlessness") had not advertised his quality by solemnly complaining of Mr. L. C. Knights' *How Many Children Had Lady Macbeth?*: "His title is misleading. He asks a question on the title-page, but never thinks to answer it."

But there is one misrepresentation that I have special reasons, relating to my part in a certain educational movement, for wishing to have corrected. "Dr. Leavis' criticism of the Cambridge English course is justified, though Mr. F. L. Lucas has stated the case better in *Cambridge University Studies,* 1933," writes your reviewer, dealing with my *How To Teach Reading.* In that pamphlet I say nothing at all about the Cambridge English course; such criticism as I offer of English courses elsewhere discriminates implicitly (as your reviewer, with a knowledge of the elementary facts, would have been aware) in favour of Cambridge. Not that I haven't criticism to offer of Cambridge English, but, from all that I hear, it would be on different lines from Mr. Lucas's.

I am, sir,

Very sincerely yours,

F. R. LEAVIS

[1] *Towards Standards of Criticism*: Selections from *The Calendar of Modern Letters* (with an introduction by Dr. Leavis). It was reviewed by Arthur Calder Marshall along with Dr. Leavis's *How to Teach Reading* and L.C. Knights' *How Many Children Had Lady Macbeth?* Mr. Calder Marshall wrote: "Dr. Leavis hints that Marxism may be necessary, so that a Communist tyranny can impose the reading of *The Calendar* on an unwilling proletariat; but suggests trying first its prescription as an educational text-book."

4. The Critic in the University
To *The Times Literary Supplement*: September 24, 1938

Sir, — The evidence of the decline of critical journalism that Mr. Middleton Murry adduces in the letter printed in your current issue (September 17) is interesting and useful; it is from his own experience and observation. But I should like to know what is the evidence on which, after noting "the almost complete disappearance of professional reviewing", he bases these remarks about the consequences:

"One that is striking is that the pressure steadily increases on those who desire seriously to pursue the profession of letters to take up teaching literature for a livelihood. That may, or may not, be a good thing for the academic study of English literature. It would need a more expert judgment than mine to pronounce on this. But I have seen no reason at all to believe that it has improved the standard of criticism: a kind of paralysis appears to descend upon the man of letters who takes to teaching literature."

I myself am convinced that it would be an extremely good thing for the academic study of English literature (and not only for that) if such "pressure" were sufficient to carry the best of such aspirants into university posts. But Mr. Murry has a very inadequate acquaintance with universities if he supposes that there is any close relation between the kind of critical intelligence he is writing about and academic success, or that the qualifications that make good critics and teachers of literature are those that win university lectureships.

To begin with, to be in the running at all for a university post one must have achieved a First Class in one's Honours examinations; and does Mr. Murry really suppose that that is a matter of having a disinterested devotion to one's subject and a first-class critical intelligence? The best that can be said is that lively critical intelligence does now and then contrive to combine itself with the ability to achieve success in the examination-room. But if Mr. Murry thinks that the possession of such intelligence is commonly found to be a recommendation when posts are being appointed to, he is astonishingly innocent about the academic mind. In the sciences no doubt things are different; for in the sciences there are real standards which cannot be altogether lost sight of. But in the humanities. . .

These comments seemed to me to be worth making because I think it of the utmost importance that the universities should (is it possible?)

be persuaded to take a serious view of their function in the modern world, and I find confirmation in Mr. Murry's evidence. I leave him to reflect, and to make inquiries of such intelligent young men as he may know who have read English or other humane subjects at any university. In any case I intend no discourtesy when I say that it is absurd to suggest that the "man of letters" on whom "a kind of paralysis appears to descend" when "he takes to teaching literature" is a critic spoiled by teaching. What critics have ever been allowed to teach?

I am, sir,
Very sincerely yours,
F. R. LEAVIS

5. In Defence of "East Coker"

To *The Times Literary Supplement*: September 21, 1940

Sir, — Mr. Eliot needs no defending, nor do I flatter myself that I am the defender he would choose if he needed one. But as a matter of decency there ought to be some protest against the review of "East Coker" that appears in your issue of yesterday, and I am writing in case no one whose protest would carry more weight has written and made my protest unnecessary.

If your reviewer had pronounced the technique of "East Coker" not altogether successful, or made limiting judgments of value in respect of the mood expressed in the poem, there would have been no call to do more than agree or disagree. What is not permissible in a serious critical journal is to write in contemptuous condescension of the greatest living English poet (what other poet have we now Yeats is gone?) and exhibit a complacent ignorance of the nature of his genius and of the nature of the technique in which that genius is manifested.[1] If "East Coker" were an experiment on unprecedented lines your reviewer would have had some excuse. But the work of a decade and a half has led directly up to it, and it is some years since another critic thought it witty to express his contempt for "Ash-Wednesday" in a parody entitled "Cinder-Thursday". Your reviewer no doubt feels himself superior in sophistication to the parodist, but his commentary is not at a higher level.

As he himself observes, the cult of Mr. Eliot has carried with it a great deal of snobbery. Now that fashion has shifted, some arbiters of taste of a kind familiar in Combination (or Common) Rooms — arbiters who know what poetry is and (as one of them has pronounced) believe that "a line scans when, without any straining of the words or melody, it can be sung to an easy and popular tune" — have found courage to expose themselves as your reviewer did and show that they have never been impressed by this unintelligible stuff. The present seems to me a

[1] The reviewer wrote: "The poets of the nineties wanted to purify poetry of all that was not poetry. Mr. Eliot's aim seems to be to purify poetry of all that is poetry." Dr. Leavis reviewed "East Coker" in *The Cambridge Review* February 21 1941, and again in an essay entitled "Eliot's Later Poetry", reprinted in *Education and the University*, (Chatto and Windus, 1943).

peculiarly unhappy time for such an exhibition in *The Times Literary Supplement*: our riches of spirit are surely not so superabundant that we can countenance it.

I am, sir,

Very sincerely yours,

F. R. LEAVIS

6. A Distinguished Book on *Paradise Lost* and its Critics
To *The Times Literary Supplement*: November 22, 1947

Sir, – More than one serious view of Mr. A.J.A. Waldock's *"Paradise Lost" and its Critics,* noticed at length in your issue of November 1 under the heading "The New Miltonians" is clearly possible, and I should not think myself justified in writing merely in order to say that I disagreed with your reviewer. I write because I am shocked by a treatment that seems to me unworthy of the best traditions of *The Times Literary Supplement.* Anyone taking his impression from your notice would dismiss the book as something he need bother about no further; the jeering and misleading kind of summary to which your reviewer confines himself has the effect of gibbeting Mr. Waldock as pretentious, ludicrous and negligible. I have read *"Paradise Lost" and its Critics* twice and am convinced that any candid reader must find it remarkable for its modesty, its patent disinterestedness and the quietly challenging force of its argument. Whether or not one agrees with Mr. Waldock is another matter; I myself have some differences to register. But I feel bound to express my conviction that he has written a distinguished book which no one interested in Milton ought to miss.

I had better, perhaps, add that I have never met Mr. Waldock and know nothing about him.

I am, sir,
Very sincerely yours,
F. R. LEAVIS

7. The Early and Late Versions of *Roderick Hudson*
To *The Times Literary Supplement*: February 12, 1949

Sir, — I am grateful to the writer of the article, "Henry James Reprints" in your issue of February 5 for pointing out that the passage from *Roderick Hudson* quoted in *The Great Tradition* comes from the late revised version. I will not occupy your space with explanations of how, though I had notes of the kinds of change in local expression revealed by comparison between the early and late versions of the book, I failed to substitute the early version of the passage I use for the extract provisionally made from the only version of *Roderick Hudson* actually in my possession. I am the more grateful to your critic because (in spite of his apparent implication) the early version suits my argument even better. In it the relation to Dickens is even plainer, and, while the betraying element of caricature is not treated to the sophisticated elaboration of the late revising hand, the effect none the less differs unmistakably from any that could have been produced by Dickens, and differs in the ways I indicate in my book.

As for the date when *Roderick Hudson* was written, I confess that I have done no original research into that: I took the date I give from the introductory note to the Chiltern Library reprint, which came to hand as I was going through my typescript.

I am, sir,
Very sincerely yours,
F. R. LEAVIS

8. The Critical Indisposition of Mr Hough
To *The New Statesman*: April 23, 1949

Sir, – Mr. Graham Hough, writing on Henry James in the current issue of *The New Statesman and Nation,* does me the honour to mention a recent book of mine. Referring to *The Bostonians,* he says:

> "He [the writer of this letter] and his author alike only miss out one thing – the essential vileness of the situation that the novel describes, the possession of a young girl by a ghastly intellectual harpy. James remains singularly complaisant about all this. He presents the hideous emotional bullying by which Verena Tarrant is enslaved with consummate skill, but he does not appear to think it particularly remarkable or ugly."

It seems to me that anyone who can say that James is complaisant in presenting the situation between Olive Chancellor and Verena Tarrant, or that he does not appear to think it particularly remarkable or ugly, or that he finds in Verena's escape "only a doubtful subject of congratulation," cannot in any serious sense have read James's book, even if he has turned over most of the pages; and I think it regrettable that yet another critic who shows a patent indisposition to be interested in James should have offered to write about him. It matters less that Mr. Hough should misrepresent me, and that, in turning over the pages of *The Great Tradition,* he should, apparently, have missed, among others, the passage in which I remark on the reasons for Miss Rebecca West's inability to forgive James's treatment of feminism (see p. 135). Or is it just possible that, in the course of his unimpressed perusal, the gist of what I say lodged in Mr. Hough's mind, and was disguised from his recognition when he came to write it down by the difference between his idiom and mine? I myself, I grant, do not use the phrases "essential vileness" or "ghastly intellectual harpy." (Mr. Hough might be judged to be an even ruggeder moralist than myself.)

In the same way, he might have made his criticism of James's "country house" by quoting from my book (the usefully compact footnote on page 172, for instance, would have served his turn very well – in so far, that is, as it was James he was concerned to discredit). As for the point that the house in *The Portrait of a Lady* belongs to an American family, I own that when *I* make it I am not making a point against America. And in general, his attention being called to places in my book from which it might plausibly be suggested that he had learnt something, Mr. Hough would no doubt reply that I, unlike him,

35

"hedge": that is, I see James's attitudes in the matter of the country house and "civilization" as decidedly complex — in ways in which, in a careful consideration of different works, I try to bring out. Moreover, James changed. And why Mr. Hough should say that I "hedge" in my strictures on the famous late novels I do not know. It is true that I find failure less accompanied by evidence of genius in one than in another. That, I suppose, gives Mr. Hough — whose criticism of *The Golden Bowl* might reasonably be taken to be a summary of mine — the opportunity to feel that he is audaciously original and outspoken in pronouncing against them all (as I do, unequivocally, myself).

I am, sir,

Very sincerely yours,

F. R. LEAVIS

9. *Scrutiny*, the British Council, the B.B.C. and Contemporary Culture

To *The Manchester Guardian*: December 15, 1953

Sir, — I suppose I ought to be grateful to Dr. Daiches for committing himself in to-day's *Manchester Guardian* to so unprecedented a public recognition (unprecedented, I mean, as coming from a senior representative of literary studies in this ancient university) that *Scrutiny* has existed, and played a major part in contemporary literary criticism. But he has made it plain that in referring thus to very relevant facts I shall be taken to confirm his implied diagnosis of persecution-mania. And in support of such a diagnosis he might very well invoke — he is, I think, actually invoking — your correspondent's note, with its most unfortunate effect of travesty ("Dr Leavis assails the Bureaucrats"), that appeared in *The Manchester Guardian* for December 4. The matter has an importance far transcending any that may be attributed to my own feelings and reputation; so I hope you will allow me space for some necessary corrective observations.

I do not, then, in my valedictory article, or anywhere, speak of any "conspiracy" against myself; and to speak of "conspiracy", in any case, is to ignore (as Dr Daiches follows all the precedents in doing) the actual analysis that has been presented and documented again and again in *Scrutiny* — the analysis of the state of literary culture in this phase of our civilization. I have not accused the British Council of enmity towards *Scrutiny* or myself. What I have said is that, as things are, an organisation financed by the State for the promotion of British culture will inevitably work to impose the social-personal "currency values of metropolitan literary society and the associated University milieux" as the distinctions and achievements of contemporary England, and so to repress the stir of genuine life. Of this truth, I have pointed out, those British Council "Surveys" present unanswerable and readily accessible evidence.

That the prevailing state of affairs has involved discrimination against *Scrutiny* no one who considers the plain facts can deny. Many people (to adduce a clear representative instance) have copies — I enclose one, sir, — of the correspondence I had with the Editor of *The Times Literary Supplement* in 1950, when a special "Survey of Contemporary British Writing for Overseas Readers" included an otherwise very comprehensive account of "Literary Periodicals" in which there was no

37

mention of *Scrutiny*. My letter calling attention to the fact was not published. A short while before that a Third Programme talk on the literary reviews of our time by Mr Pryce-Jones had also, though it ranged from *New Verse* to *The Criterion,* left out *Scrutiny.* Mr John Raymond in a later talk on contemporary literary criticism achieved a similar discrimination: it has, in fact, been routine. And I am surprised that Dr Daiches, after his participation in a fairly recent series of talks on "Literary Criticism in Our Time", feels himself able to report a general readiness in B.B.C. performers to recognise, on the due occasion, any such order of achievement as he has just attributed to *Scrutiny* and *Scrutiny* authors in your pages.

I am surprised, too, that he should be able to feel that he knows of no discrimination in the academic world. Of many relevant facts I will produce only this: two of the major Cambridge bookshops, in deference to what they took to be authoritative influences, refused to stock *Scrutiny.*

I have tried to indicate in a limited space that the case about the state of contemporary criticism tacitly dismissed by Dr Daiches is a formidable one, and has been presented very fully in *Scrutiny.* No one has ever attempted to answer it. If it is true, at the lowest level of consideration those who live on literature have reason to reflect whether their host may not be in danger of dying under them. And it seems to me a peculiarly unworthy tactic to dismiss such a case with a personal imputation – in the very nature of such a matter very readily taken up – of persecution-mania.

And finally let me remind Dr Daiches that the "literature of mere entertainment" and the "urbane cultivation of letters", to which he thinks *Scrutiny* has failed to give a due appreciation, have in our time been academically hall-marked with degrees, honoris causa, at our ancient universities.

I am, sir,
Very sincerely yours,
F. R. LEAVIS

10. Hawthorne and Melville

To *The Times Literary Supplement*: May 21, 1954

Sir, — In the article "American Perspectives" in your last issue I read: "Cooper and Hawthorne are not great novelists, but considered with Melville and Henry James, they reveal, as Dr. F.R. Leavis and Mr. Marius Bewley have pointed out, qualities which mark them out as being highly important in the development of the modern novel." I write because I should not like the view of Hawthorne as "not a great novelist" to be taken as mine (or Mr. Bewley's, for I am sure that he too would wish to disclaim it). Hawthorne seems to me one of the most astonishingly original writers in the English language, and if he had not been profound as well as successful in his originality — if the themes and interests that impelled his innovations in the art of fiction had not been major in their human significance — he could not have had the profound influence on Henry James that he actually had. By what canons of "greatness" in a novelist can greatness be denied the author of *The Scarlet Letter, My Kinsman Major Molineux, Young Goodman Brown,* and *The Maypole of Merrymount*? The account of these works that I should appeal to in order to enforce my challenge, if enforcement were required, can be found in an essay by Q. D. Leavis that appeared, under the title "Hawthorne as Poet", in the *Sewanee Review* for Spring and for Summer, 1951.[1]

It is surely time that Hawthorne was recognized as without question one of the great masters. I will add that it seems to me as absurd to couple James with Melville as Hawthorne with Cooper. Of course, it may not have been your essayist's intention to imply that James and Melville are comparable magnitudes. But he certainly implies that Melville comes under the description, "great novelist", from which Hawthorne is to be excluded. It seems to me, then, that in solid and significant achievement Hawthorne is much more securely a great writer than Melville.

I am, sir,

Very sincerely yours,

F. R. LEAVIS

---

[1] Mrs. Leavis's study of Hawthorne was reprinted in the volume of critical essays on Hawthorne edited by G.N. Kaul in the Twentieth Century Views series, published in America by Prentice-Hall.

11. The Right Approach to Shakespeare
To *The Times Literary Supplement*: July 9, 1954

Sir, — I have hesitated before again writing to correct what amounts to the imputation of a critical position to me that I have never held; yet if my views are thought worth referring to, I may properly insist, perhaps, on what they are and what they are not. And I do think the question of the right approach to Shakespeare an important one. The writer of the article, "Shakespeare's Craft of Verse," in your issue of July 2 suggests that, in my discussion of the character of Othello as "real" (his word), I expose a critical inconsistency that is inherent in my approach to Shakespeare. Developing the point, he (or she) sees the difference between Professor Empson's discussion of *Measure for Measure* and mine as being that Professor Empson, "Like Bradley, or the plain man, or the audience in a theatre, cannot help considering the situation as 'actual' and the characters as 'real'."

Without, it seems, appreciating the significance of his doing so, your reviewer helpfully puts "actual" and "real" in inverted commas. The theatre audience at a performance of *Othello* that should, in responding to the two main characters as real and the murder as actual, have done so by calling for the police, or rising and rushing on the stage, or producing revolvers and shooting Mr. Paul Robeson, would have behaved with pre-critical crudity: your reviewer, with his inverted commas, is implicitly recognizing this truth. He is implicitly recognizing the difficulties and complexities inhering in his terms "actual" and "real" (difficulties and complexities that he must surely in his undergraduate days have discussed in connexion with Dr. Johnson's: "The truth is, the spectators are always in their senses. . ."). If I agree, or assert (as I do), that in responding to a Shakespeare play that engages us imaginatively we respond *as if* the situations were actual and the characters real, I go on to insist that the "as if" must be understood to have an essential qualifying value: it registers the fact that, in responding, we at the same time know that this is *not* actual life, so that our response is, in various ways, different from what it would be in dealing in actual life with such situations as are represented. The value of the "as if" (to use a shorthand compelled upon me by the need for brevity) varies from play to play, and even from point to point within a play. The importance of this truth, surely is one of the first things one learns in learning to read Shakespeare critically.

We can determine the precise value on any occasion only by attending sensitively and intelligently to the organization of words that Shakespeare has left us with. I have myself said, in the essay to which your reviewer refers, that, of all Shakespeare's major plays, *Othello* seems to me the one answering most nearly to Bradley's notion of poetic drama. It is something very close to a realistic novel in dramatic form; and corresponding criteria of psychological realism apply in the criticism of it: we judge Othello as we should judge someone we knew in life. If we decide that Othello's behaviour is not, by those criteria, adequately motivated, or that Othello in the real life that we know would not have acted in that way, then we pass a severe adverse criticism on the play. But the tragedy is very much the tragedy of the Moor Othello. And I suggest that if, responding sensitively to the dramatic poem. we appreciate the sense in which this is so, we perceive that Iago is an accessory character, and needs only to be (as he is) immediately convincing: on critical reflection we realize, if not incapacitated by false assumptions, that the focus should be on Othello and on the tragedy inherent in Othello's character and situation. To give the space that Bradley does to finding motives for Iago, and to "appreciating" him as an historical character (who can be compared with Napoleon) is ridiculous. Nor is it intelligent to make it a *donnée* about Othello that he is a poet (he speaks poetry), or to expend energy on theories of "double time." Whether I am right or wrong, this is what I have in fact contended.

As for *Measure for Measure* (which is a very different kind of play from *Othello*, and, in my view, a much greater), I think it especially deplorable that your reviewer should, in relation to that play, reduce the possibilities to "Bradley's method used with tact" and something called "the method of symbolic analysis." What the latter may be I do not know, but I cannot suppose that any approach that seemed to me intelligent would be a fair target for that description. On the other hand, if "tact" could be supposed to mean a duly intelligent and informed concern for truth of response to the actual concrete work in front of one, then I should say I was in favour of "tact"; but I think that "tact", so interpreted, would turn "Bradley's method" into something that it would be as absurd to call *that* as it would be to call it the "method of symbolic analysis."

I am, sir,

Very sincerely yours,

F. R. LEAVIS

12. The Complex Fate

To *The Times Literary Supplement*: October 1, 1954

Sir, – In the "additional pages" on "American Writing To-day," going with your issue for September 17, a contributor refers (p. xxxvi) to James's "classic pronouncement": "It's a complex fate being an American. . ." If the particular pronouncement has some currency as "classic", that, it seems to me, is due to Mr. Marius Bewley, whose book, *The Complex Fate,* came out two years ago, and treats with great penetration and suggestiveness the theme of your contributor's article. At any rate, I write because Mr. Bewley's book is nowhere, I think, mentioned either in your additional hundred pages or in the rest of the issue, and yet Mr. Bewley ought to be known in this country as one of the most distinguished, and most enlightening, American critics now writing – and his book, being published on this side, is very accessible. He seems to me one of the best critics now using the English language.

I am, sir,
Very sincerely yours,
F. R. LEAVIS

13. Mr Pritchett's Tropes
To *The New Statesman*: December 11, 1954

Sir, – Mr. V.S. Pritchett, reviewing Professor Tillotson's *Thackeray the Novelist,* writes: "It is not enough to be pained by Dr. Leavis's telling Thackeray to leave the room because he is only a greater Trollope – quite a good throwaway line for the classroom; what is important is to say that teacher left out half the English tradition and tried to rebuild the English novel by putting the roof of Henry James on first." Are we to conclude from this assured and vivacious pronouncement (it may not be addressed to the "classroom", but it has the air of relying confidently on the right response from the "boys") that Mr. Pritchett thinks it silly to make critical distinctions within the field of prose fiction? He himself goes on to say: "There is a comic, loose-knit, sentimental and diffuse tradition, and Thackeray must be judged within it."

To say that Thackeray "must be judged within it" is to say that he must, for critical purposes, be dismissed *to* it from the company in which Professor Tillotson would place him. The novels of Jane Austen, Hawthorne, George Eliot and Henry James are *not* loose-knit, sentimental or diffuse; in the interest of significance that could not otherwise have been conveyed, they are closely organised – organised in ways that relate them to the mature plays of Shakespeare. I have, in the book to which Mr. Pritchett refers, and elsewhere, given grounds for holding that the authors (together with some others) form a tradition it is important to distinguish. That I am wrong, or that Thackeray belongs to it, nothing said by Mr. Pritchett (or Professor Tillotson) seems to me to go any way towards showing. I do not question that my own careful and detailed argument might be subjected to criticism from which, as a critic, I should benefit; but Mr. Pritchett's tropes, and the all-too-familiar kind of routine sneer in which he indulges, do not seem to me to be criticism, or to advance in any way the business of critical thought.

As for Thackeray, there is another distinction to be made in regard to him; it was made by Dickens, the creator of Henry Gowan. Dickens disliked Thackeray, not as a formidable competitor, but as a very influential writer who was cynical about his art, and who thus, while enjoying the profits and the prestige it brought him, used his influence to discredit the novelist's art in general.

I am, sir,

Very sincerely yours,

F. R. LEAVIS

14. In Defence of *Scrutiny*

To *The London Magazine*: March 1955

Sir, — If I tell Mr L.D. Lerner that I cannot see why he should pay *Scrutiny* such high compliments when he does what he can to discredit and defeat its essential purpose — when he shows a blind hostility to the function it served — he will no doubt feel that I am making him a characteristically furious answer. I refer to his article, 'The Life and Death of *Scrutiny*', in *The London Magazine* for January. It is of no use, I know, to *tell* him that there is nothing like fury in my present state, and that I think he does something worse than commit a personal injustice at my expense (a minor matter) when he passes on that charge of 'bad-tempered'. Instead I will ask him to ask himself how he came, in the opening of his article, to be guilty of so undeniable and large an untruth as to say that the Epilogue to the new edition of my *New Bearings* 'is in fact a discussion of the reception and influence of the first edition of the book'.

The Epilogue, 'in fact', explains at length why I don't, as Mr Lerner registers, pick up my discussion of modern poetry and add a section on what has been written since 1932. The explanation has its focus in the case of Auden, the one notable talent of the 'Poetic Renascence'. I take Auden's as the type-career of the 1930s and a portent. The swift 'arrival', the acceptance of the star-turn aplomb of an undergraduate-coterie hero as the creative brilliance of a major poet, the continued failure to mature — we have here, I point out, the clear manifestation of a portentous lapse of standards.

It is only in a coherent, educated and influential reading-public, one capable of responding intelligently and making its response felt, that standards are 'there' for the critic to appeal to: only where there is such a public can he invoke them with any effect. A great fact of the literary history of our time is that such a public no longer exists. The fact is manifested in the difficulty of establishing and keeping alive any serious critical organ. It is manifested in the characteristic uncertainty of tone of Auden's verse, which seems to offer itself to a *public* public, and yet confuses that public with the Group, the coterie, from the consciousness of solidarity with which it draws the confidence for its callow sophistication. Auden's success was a disaster for any talent he may have had, and his career illustrates the consequences for literature of a state of affairs in which the natural tendency of a small modish literary

44

world to impose its social-personal valuations as those of serious criticism remains unchecked. For if it is a small world, it is, as a system of personal and institutional connections, comprehensive: it virtually controls the currency of accepted valuations and the climate of taste. Since its *raison d'être* is to ensure the kudos (not to speak of the profits) of literary distinction against exposure to standards, it is inevitably disastrous for English literature, in the present and the future. Standards having been once banished, such a system will resist with all its resources the reinstatement of the offensive presence.

Why does Mr Lerner ignore these contentions in his account of my Epilogue, though they form its main substance and explain why the post-Eliot history of English poetry should be so discouraging — so discouraging that it couldn't be dealt with by taking up again the critical approach of *New Bearings*? Is it because they are patently untrue and groundless? Because no informed and intelligent person knows of any evidence that could give them colour, or make them anything but wholly improbable imaginings?

The effect of such a state of affairs on those who have known nothing different, and (a very general consequence) cannot believe that there ever has been, or could be, anything essentially different, is illustrated by Mr Lerner. He has, it seems, read some of the criticism devoted to Auden in *Scrutiny,* but he might as well not have read it, since he ignores entirely what it says. More than half-a-dozen critics, representing a wide variety of background and personality, reviewed Auden, and they concurred substantially in judgement. This criticism is carefully argued, it is specific and detailed in formulation; it makes its force plain and it produces its grounds. But Mr Lerner pays it no attention; he seems unable to realize that it *is* criticism — or to realize what criticism is. The reviewers, he complains, are niggling, ungracious and ungrateful; they ought to have said how much they enjoyed Auden, and to have devoted their reviews mainly to developing *that* theme. He cannot, it seems, grasp that the criticism of Auden is not that ('perhaps', Mr Lerner puts it) 'he is not as great as Eliot', but that for those who are capable of appreciating the difference between the two, Auden can yield no satisfaction at all; he can only bore and exasperate. He could be taken for a poet of satisfying creative achievement only by those who are so much of the cultural conditions he represents that they cannot criticize them — they cannot believe them to be new and unprecedented.

Actually Mr Lerner is a little out-of-date; criticism and the facts have at last told, and Auden has been virtually abandoned: even in *The Times Literary Supplement* we are unlikely to hear much more of him as a great poet. Mr Lerner, if he wanted the cogent force that derives from fashionable unanimity would have done better to confine himself to Dylan Thomas, *Scrutiny*'s shameful obtuseness in respect of whom is for the moment the favoured illustration. However, he shouldn't rely on its being found so telling in four or five years' time. And meanwhile it surprises me that he can suppose he adds plausibility to his case by adducing (in association with the 'Eliot of the plays and the later prose') Graham Greene and Christopher Fry as unquestionable shining distinctions of the age and clear victims of *Scrutiny*'s 'grudging attitude towards its contemporaries'. Even the appreciation of L.H. Myers in *Scrutiny* was grudging, according to Mr Lerner, though I myself should have said that it illustrated *Scrutiny*'s readiness to salute what was salutable, and that the charge might more reasonably be that the discussion of Myers's distinctive interest as a writer for the intelligent could be taken to imply a higher estimate of him as a novelist, a creative writer, than could be critically sustained.

If *Scrutiny* failed to perform the critical function in relation to the literature of its own time, what, in Mr Lerner's view, did it do to earn his qualified good opinion? He gives an astonishing account of a kind of criticism he calls 'practical criticism' and attributes to the critics who wrote for *Scrutiny*. He derives this 'practical criticism' from 'Eliot, Graves, Richards, Middleton Murry, and the American New Critics'. '*Scrutiny*', he says, 'set out from the beginning to apply their methods, not sporadically but systematically, over the whole field of English Literature'. I will not comment on the details of this list of alleged models, except to remark that there is no American critic, I think, and certainly no one at all with a knowledge of relevant chronological facts and historical possibilities, who wouldn't, if the question of influence were thought worth discussing, reverse Mr Lerner's suggestion regarding the relation between *Scrutiny* and the 'New Criticism' (to say which is not to claim any credit − or to admit responsibility). What I *must* comment on is that conception of 'practical criticism' (if it can be called a conception) which Mr Lerner offers to define. The term, which I have never liked, imposes itself, if at all, as an academic convenience: it means, in common acceptance, elementary exercises in judgment and analysis, the specimens, in the nature of the conditions of work, necessarily being as a rule short poems or passages. One reason for my disliking it is that it encourages the kind of confusion into which Mr Lerner is led

46

IN DEFENCE OF *SCRUTINY*

when he elaborates his antithesis of 'practical' and 'theoretical'.

If he looks again, for instance, at the essay of mine to which he refers, he will see how completely he misrepresents me about Coleridge. I do indeed use the phrase 'practical criticism', but it is with the reverse of the intention he ascribes to me. I am preoccupied in that essay with questioning the implications of 'theoretical' as it takes the stress in the accepted account of Coleridge – with questioning, in fact, the implications of Mr Lerner's antithesis, which is the antithesis invoked when we are told that Coleridge is the great master of *theoretical* criticism. I point out that, in the places that seem to me to manifest Coleridge's distinctive genius as a critic most clearly and notably (and I specify chapter XV of *Biographia Literaria,* and of that chapter the second head above all), it is impossible to disengage the dealings with principle from the 'practical criticism'. We realize in such places, I remark, that the ' "master of theoretical criticism" who matters is the completion of a practical critic'. I remark this of Coleridge, but the proposition can be taken as general, and it cuts, of course, both ways. If I cannot imagine a great master of such critical theory as matters who is not a great critic – a great critic in critical practice, neither can I imagine a great or considerable critic who is not very much concerned with critical principle.

And I cannot imagine a great or considerable critic who is not very much concerned with 'fundamentals' in a wider sense than 'critical principle' may suggest. What the context is of the sentence of Walton's quoted by Mr Lerner I don't know, but Mr Lerner's ability to suppose that the sentence, with the force he gives it, conveys a maxim that could have governed the criticism in *Scrutiny* only illustrates the incapacitating power of his preconceptions. 'And in the end,' he says, 'Coleridge is a greater critic than anyone who wrote for *Scrutiny* because he is both a practical critic and also prepared – and able – to discuss fundamentals.'

I don't need to take up Mr Lerner's comparative judgment in order to reply that no body of criticism has been more concerned with discussing fundamentals than that which appeared in *Scrutiny.* He is able, paradoxically (in view of the high compliments he pays), to believe the opposite, or something like it, because he assumes that the type of any serious discussion of fundamentals must be the philosophical. So strong is this assumption that he can read my essay on Coleridge without registering its main preoccupation, which is to show that Coleridge's effective dealings with critical principle come from the critic, and not from the philosopher and metaphysician, and are to be found, not in the

47

formulations that invite us to discuss how far they are original, and how far they may be indebted to one or more of the German idealists, but in the criticism that could have been written only by an English literary critic – a writer born to the English language, inward with English poetry, and practised in its analysis. Similarly, Mr Lerner seems not to have noticed that, in the reply to Dr Wellek he refers to, so far from disclaiming any interest in defining the criteria and grounds of my criticism, I point out that they are defined in the actual process of the criticism with a precision (it seems to me) that makes the kind of defining Dr Wellek favours intolerably clumsy and ineffective. My reply to Mr Robert Wagner, the nature of which again escapes Mr Lerner, is closely related. I wished to convey to Mr Wagner that it was *he* who in effect was refusing to discuss fundamentals. I intimated that he couldn't expect his very large gestures towards Plato, Aristotle, Leibnitz and Spinoza to be taken seriously while he showed, where creative literature was in question, what I can only call a complacent illiteracy and refused to read Lawrence – refused to believe that the reading of Lawrence *could* be something different from recognizing illustrations of familiar ideas; must be, in fact, a matter of living into a profound mode of original thought.

The conception, then, of literary criticism shared, in their very various ways, by the writers who collaborated in *Scrutiny* was very different from what Mr Lerner propounds. It was a conception, certainly, of the critic's business as being to maintain a disciplined fidelity to the, work in front of him; but of criticism as being *therefore* a specific discipline of thought, concerned essentially with fundamentals. Mr Lerner won't, I hope, put it down to my characteristic bad temper when I say that, though he says some flattering things about me, he doesn't – what would have tended more to gratify me – recognize the kind of closely organized and scrupulously defining thought aimed at in my criticism. Thus, referring to the essay on 'Mr Eliot and Milton' in *The Common Pursuit,* he 'replies' to my observations about Milton's imagery without paying any attention to the context, as if *they,* in their dislocated state, might fairly be taken as representing my case about Milton. He doesn't notice that they are offered as developing certain points about the Miltonic habit conceded by Mr Eliot, and that they have their intended significance as forming part of a closely organized argument – an argument that involves a great deal else besides imagery and must be considered as a whole.

I must lay one further emphasis regarding the preoccupation of any serious criticism with fundamentals, and as a reminder of the way in which literary-critical thinking is governed by radical 'value-judgments'. I can do it by quoting a passage in which Lawrence defines the spirit in which he reads and judges contemporary literature (he is thinking of the novel as, before all others, the potentially significant mode):

> "Supposing a bomb were put under the whole scheme of things, what would we be after? What feelings do we want to carry through to the next epoch? What feelings will carry us through? What is the underlying impulse in us that will provide the motive power for a new state of things when this democratic-industrial-lovey-dovey-darling-take-me-to-mamma state of things is bust?"

It is in creative literature that one finds the challenge to discover what one's real beliefs and values are (they are not a matter of propositions — or answers to propositions — about the teaching of Plato, Aristotle, Leibnitz and Spinoza). It follows that it is of great importance to have a contemporary literature and — for there will not long be a literature where there is no intelligent public — to have a serious contemporary criticism. To have this is to have a serious criticism of the past — of the past, inevitably, in relation to the present. Mr Lerner's ability to see *Scrutiny*'s dealings with the past as the establishing of a list of 'heroes' goes with his blindness to the function of criticism as it bears on the present.

Any resolute attempt to assert the critical function so conceived must, in the nature of things, have met, any time in the past quarter of a century, with an intense general hostility. If I insist on such hostility as a major fact in the history of *Scrutiny,* there is another reason than the defect of personal temper that Mr Lerner deplores (tolerantly). It is given in his ability to suggest that the fact may be questioned, or dismissed as of little significance. Is one to suppose his acquaintance with the English literary and academic scenes so recent, or his interest in them so slight, that he *can* honestly question the fact? There *has,* it is true, in the past year, been a good deal of recognition that *Scrutiny* once existed and played an important part in literary history. But it is precisely for a year that *Scrutiny* has been dead. And till it died the review that Mr Lerner pronounces necessary was (except for sneers and cocksnooks) denied virtually all recognition — denied it by a unanimity of the powers controlling literary opinion. The spirit of the literary world may be fairly represented by those compliments, paid habitually, in broadcast talks and in print, to the American quarterlies — serious critical reviews that we on this side (it seemed) couldn't rival. Such was the hostility that the English literary world preferred to suppress the achievement of its own country, and deny one clear superiority that England (it is now pretty generally granted in both countries) could have claimed. Did Mr Lerner never hear or read any of those surveys, in broadcast talks and in *The Times Literary Supplement,* which, going through the literary journals and reviews, omitted regularly *one*; omitted — it was a matter of establised convention — all references to *Scrutiny?* If he has any doubt about the record of *The Times Literary Supplement,* let him look through its files for the past ten years (to stimulate his researches I am sending him a copy of some correspondence I had two or three years ago with the editor). All the collaborators in *Scrutiny,* it is relevant to note, were unpaid; the whole enterprise depended on personal devotion; and no one supposed that to be associated with *Scrutiny* was the best way of ensuring a prosperous academic career. The effect of the general denial of recognition was to give the inevitable hostility of the academic world (Mr Lerner thinks of *Scrutiny* as 'an appendage of Cambridge') a confident strength and persistence it wouldn't otherwise have had, and the ultimate consequence was the death of *Scrutiny.*

What I am pointing out is that Mr Lerner's complete lack of interest in the causes of the death goes with his inability to understand the achievement, and consequently with his lack of interest in the conditions of the life. He has no notion of the intensity and kind of effort that went to establishing and maintaining *Scrutiny,* and consequently no notion — though he says *Scrutiny* is 'necessary' — of the effort and resolution that would be required to achieve anything of the same order again. He says lightly that 'most of its leading critics have now made their names and can probably find other channels for their work'. Where? And how does he suppose they came to write, and in a way of which (on the whole) he approves? Does he think it was merely a matter of there being some vehicle to hand that would carry what they might happen to find themselves writing?

I have been at pains to deal seriously with his misrepresentations and misconceptions because (to take up his 'necessary') it is now *desperately* necessary that the function of criticism should be restored. There can be no hope of that while the nature of the function is forgotten, and the completeness of the lapse unrecognized. Matthew Arnold, eighty years ago, feared that England would decline into a larger Holland, and said that he would rather not live to see it. It sounds today, whatever he may have meant, like an insult to Holland. Acute as he was, his prevision was mercifully limited. Today we have to fear that the country that in its time produced Shakespeare, George Eliot and Lawrence ('England my England!') has become, irretrievably, the country of the Welfare State, the Football Pools, and the literary culture of the *New Statesman* and the Third Programme.

I am, sir,

Very sincerely yours,

F. R. LEAVIS

15. *Puddn'head Wilson* and *Those Extraordinary Twins*
To *Commentary*: May 1956

Sir, – I did indeed know of *Those Extraordinary Twins*, but I do not agree that it and *Puddn'head Wilson* constitute together an "Italian freak."[1] Nor, in my opinion, do the facts that Miss Pierce presents tend in any way either to prove me wrong, or to show (even if facts of that kind could) that *Puddn'head Wilson* is a patchwork. On the contrary, I find nothing but confirmation in her scholarship. "But. . . other people began intruding themselves": this is a note, not (surely!) on the botching up of a patchwork, but on the genesis of an inspired work of imagination, a living thing (I need not remind Miss Pierce of the more famous cases of the kind). Wilson, Roxy, and Tom Driscoll, she says, "took over the story." To the inspired "tragedy" that resulted the "farce" is wholly irrelevant: there is not the slightest ground for contradicting Mark Twain's judgment. To *Puddn'head Wilson* there is no farcical aspect, and nothing approaching one (unless for prisoners of the convention that twins are *intrinsically* farcical).

I wish that *Those Extraordinary Twins* could have been – could be – forgotten: its association with the other tale about twins has certainly played its part in the neglect of a classic of the English language. That *Puddn'head Wilson* is such is, of course, not a fact of scholarship, but a critical judgment, and a critical judgment cannot be coercively demonstrated. Pointing to the essential fact, the created thing, and making the commentary that seems to one called for, one appeals, implicitly, for agreement, even though one anticipates that the responses most worth having will often be in the form "Yes, but –." I am sorry that an authority on Mark Twain should feel that, for her, there can be no "Yes" in it at all. But what I point to seems to me, still, clearly – and irresistibly – what I judged it to be.

I am, sir,

Very sincerely yours,

F. R. LEAVIS

---

[1] Miss Pierce quoted Mark Twain: "I had seen a picture of a youthful Italian 'freak' . . . and I thought I would write an extravagantly fantastic little story with this freak of nature for hero. . . . But. . . other people began intruding themselves." "I pulled out the farce and left the tragedy." Miss Pierce considered *Those Extraordinary Twins* to be the true neglected classic, and *Puddn'head Wilson* "a lightweight soap opera."

16. A New 'Establishment' in Criticism?

To *The Listener*: November 1, 1956

Sir, – Mr. Holloway's cue has been taken. It is now established that what anyone who was not a member of it would call the Establishment (if that word is to be used) is nothing of the kind, but a scattered company of free-lance pioneers who have defied the deadening power of institutional orthodoxy and carried on their lonely and challenging work in a hostile world. In a letter in *The Listener* of October 25 Mr. Paul Gardner speaks of the 'individual critics' who seem to him to have done the 'most significant work' since the 'foundation of the New Criticism' and who 'have remained quite outside the Establishment'. 'Dr. Tillyard and Professor Lewis', he goes on, by way of explaining the kind of outsider he has in mind, 'created their great body of Milton criticism in opposition to Mr. Eliot and Dr. Leavis'.

How heroic this sounds! And to me – it is of its implications in regard to myself that I am thinking – how ironical in its fantastic reversal of history (I think of the achievements of the Russian practitioners). I had meant to make no comment on Mr. Holloway's performances, but now I find myself compelled: memories are short, the resources of what *I* should call the Establishment are immense, and there is a plain duty in front of me.

No one, then, in the least acquainted with the actual history could suppose that, in the years when Dr. Tillyard and Professor Lewis were founding their reputations, they had any need to brace themselves against opposition from me or to be discouraged by the rumour of *my* disagreement. It was not merely that I had no position of power; no view associated with my name was treated with anything but the reverse of deference in any quarter where it could matter to Dr. Tillyard and Professor Lewis to have opinion with them. When *New Bearings* came out (in 1932) it was the signal for a concerted reaction of solidarity among the powers of the academic world, a reaction expressing itself, not in considered criticism, but in allusive and critically unscrupulous sneers. Anything of that kind was permissible at my expense: let Mr. Gardner and Mr. Holloway look at the inaugural lectures from the Chair of Poetry at Oxford, the Warton lectures, the British Academy lectures, and the section of Cambridge University Studies (the book came out just before the middle 'thirties) dealing with the English School. *New Bearings* got no review in the *Criterion* and my *Revaluation,* later, got a deliberately insulting dismissal; Dr. Tillyard's *Milton,* on the other

hand, received the most deferential and eulogistic of long reviews. If
Mr. Gardner and Mr. Holloway consider this matter at all important
they will find it repaying to do a little comparative research into the re-
spective treatments over the past quarter of a century, given to myself
and (say) to Dr. Tillyard in *The Times Literary Supplement,* the *New
Statesman and Nation,* the Sunday newspapers, and *The Listener.* The
comparison will leave them unable to doubt which of us belonged to
what was in every sense the Establishment and which did not. Between
1932 and 1948 my books got no review in the *New Statesman and
Nation,* though my name often appeared for derision. And the suggestion that I had any reason to think of Mr. Eliot as an ally or associate or
in any way 'on my side' must strike me as peculiarly ironical.

It was I who was the outsider – the description fairly applies. For
the first half-dozen years of *Scrutiny* I had no post and no salary, and
was hard put to it to make a living. None of the collaborators in
Scrutiny had any position or influence. Dr. Tillyard, on the other hand,
could be described by his publisher as 'the able and energetic head of
the Cambridge English School'. For the twenty years of its life *Scrutiny*
had to contend against the hostility, overt and covert, intense and
wholly unscrupulous, of the academic and literary worlds, or of what I
think it reasonable to call the Establishment – the people who had the
posts, the salaries, the positions of power, and all the means of promoting or thwarting careers and worldly success. It was the hostility of the
academic world that led to the death of *Scrutiny.* I have said this in
print before, and I am very ready to explain to Mr. Holloway, in detail
and with illustrations, what I mean by it.

He no doubt inclines to reply that, when he spoke of the 'Establishment', he had nothing in mind but some realm of intellectual fashions.
If this was really so I can only say that, for a critic offering the kind of
pretension represented by his talks, he showed a truly remarkable and
significant insensitiveness to the force, implication, and inevitable
effect of the term he chose to rely on so centrally. 'Never trust the
talker, trust the talk': I, as I read his first talk, asked myself why, proposing to deal with what may be called unfortunate derivativeness
from truly original work in criticism, he should not even have glanced
at *Poetry Direct and Oblique,*[1] which bears so obvious a relation to
Empson's earlier *Seven Types of Ambiguity* (as well as to the work of
other original critics), and which, coming from a major eminence of

[1] By Dr. Tillyard.

the Establishment (in the usual sense), is so representative and significant a case for his proposed theme. The question, of course, was rhetorical. The names he did mention as well as the names he did not made the answer plain enough.

And what, I ask, has my criticism in common with Mr. Wilson Knight's, Mr. Traversi's, Mr. Eliot's, or Professor Empson's? I can only say that to lump together half-a-dozen very individual critics and, associating them with a number of unintelligent imitators, to make of them, for poised and solemn discussion, a New Criticism (the 'Establishment'), seems to me an intellectually abject proceeding, and one *not* calculated to advance the cause of literature or critical thought. When Mr. Gardner assimilates me and (the surely very different) Mr. Eliot to *the* 'New Criticism', that characteristically American academic industry, he is acting in the spirit of Mr. Holloway's suggestion.

As for the Establishment in my (the obvious) sense of the word, it is to be seen, I should say, in those who have the institutional positions and the power in the institutional system, and, by all the signs, stand solidly together — those, for instance, who, when *The Listener* prints a Third Programme talk of theirs, get (as Mr. Holloway did for his first talk) an editorial comment at the beginning of the number saying what an important service they are performing, and an appreciative note from the official critic at the end. And if Mr. Holloway, who would find it hard to argue plausibly that he is *persona non grata* to what *I* call the Establishment, or that he knows nothing about its workings on the academic side, should suggest that to be known as a pupil of mine or an admirer of *Scrutiny* is a passport to success in an academic career, I should be obliged to say — as of course I shall not — that he was guilty of dishonesty.

Finally, let me say that if Mr. Holloway should still insist that there is some esoteric sense intended by him in which I have become the 'Establishment', that, I must reply, has been in spite of every kind of opposition on the part of the Establishment in the ordinary sense.

> I am, sir,
> Very sincerely yours,
> F. R. LEAVIS

17. The Priestley Travesty

To *The New Statesman*: December 8, 1956

Sir, — What travesty Mr. Priestley was travestying when he honoured me with his attention in your pages I didn't know; it hardly, at the time, seemed to me to matter much. When, however, in your issue of December 1, a month after Mr. Priestley's original performance, you print the letter from Mr. James Reeves I feel compelled to make some comment. Mr. Reeves doesn't convey his intention very precisely or directly (he was no doubt anxious to avoid dogmatism), but in printing his letter you implicitly offer it as a seriously relevant contribution and, I must suppose, aimed at me. "Some critics," says Mr. Reeves, "are more concerned for their professional standards than for the literature they profess to serve": they practise or preach a "dogmatic exclusiveness" — this appears to be the charge — that discourages people who haven't read anything as good as "even Mr. Priestley" from making contacts with literature they would otherwise have made. I needn't discuss how, exactly, the alleged process of discouragement could work or what conception Mr. Reeves himself can have of the function of criticism (I cannot myself see what is gained by getting one's pupils to read best-sellers). What I have to note is the pretty obvious relation of his "dogmatic exclusiveness" to the figure presented as me by Mr. Priestley.

Let me then say that, in the talk to which Mr. Priestley referred, so far from being engaged in general demolition, I was guided by the explicit aim of insisting on the different kinds of discrimination one has to make in coming to terms with the literature of one's own time. It was essentially *of* my theme that I should instance (it strikes me as odd that I should have to say this, in view of the printed evidence of my habit as a critic) a number of creative achievements that seem to me to stand as, in their different ways, classical or memorable, though not among the greatest, or even major. It is very true that I was concerned to insist on the importance of standards; I gave my grounds for holding that, in the past quarter of a century, much talent had failed to develop because of the absence of standards — because, that is, of the virtual abeyance of the critical function (and, let me say, no serious attempt has ever been made to answer the case that I have presented with a great deal of particularity, again and again). In my account of what a due performance of the function of criticism would have been like — for there you have my theme — the conception of criticism I invoked was the very reverse of a dogmatic one. Mr. R.W.H. Holland who, in another letter, alleges that for some undergraduates I tend to be an "oracle", will perhaps bear witness that the "oracle", where he is listened to, is known for his insistence that criticism, of its essential nature, is collaborative — collaborative and creative, and that a due performance of the function requires a plurality of centres. (Undergraduates making, in discussion, the point that a judgment has the form "This is so, is it not?" and that the critic expects a response of the form "Yes, but —," have been greeted with ironical smiles by colleagues of mine: the "influence" is recognised.)

I do indeed think it urgently necessary for a living contemporary literature that the function of criticism should be restored, and therefore I am depressed (if not, unhappily, surprised) when the *New Statesman and Nation* judges such an article as Mr. Priestley's a good thing for a journal that addresses an educated public to print.

I am, sir,

Very sincerely yours,

F. R. LEAVIS

18. Left Wing Intellectuals and Working Class Culture
To *The New Statesman*: March 9, 1957

Sir, — The reviewer of Mr. Richard Hoggart's *The Uses of Literacy* in your issue for March 2 attributes to me an originality, and a status as originator, for which it would be indecent in me, as well as ridiculous, to accept the credit. He speaks of "Dr. Leavis, Denys Thompson and their followers" and says that *Culture and Environment* was Mr. Hoggart's "starting-point." But I (along with Mr. Thompson) am as properly to be called a follower as Mr. Hoggart himself is. I wrote *Culture and Environment* in a week (with Mr. Thompson to advise me as to tact and tactics from the schoolmaster's point of view), and I was able to do so because the real work had all been done. The material I arranged to form that opuscule was taken from the documentation accumulated for *Fiction and the Reading Public,* a massive thoroughly documented and argued study already published, and one in which I can claim no part. Your reviewer speaks of Dr. Leavis and Denys Thompson as "concentrating upon the effects of advertising and mass production." But *Fiction and the Reading Public* was very far from offering the limited scope suggested by that account of *Culture and Environment.* The product of a wholly original kind of research, it was a "socio-literary study" that did indeed "break new ground" and introduce new ideas and new methods: among other things it made a pioneering inquiry into the old working-class culture of which the new processes of civilization were eliminating the traces — an inquiry that was greeted with angry contempt by Harold Laski and the left-wing intellectuals of the nineteen-thirties.

The quoted phrases in my last sentence come from your review of Mr. Hoggart's book. I make this point because your review of *Fiction and the Reading Public* a quarter of a century ago was headed "Best-sellers Massacred" and carried out in that spirit: it contained not the slightest hint that any sociological intention or interest might be found in the book under review (and *Culture and Environment* a little later was dismissed in the *New Statesman and Nation* with a contemptuous paragraph). Your reviewer says that Mr. Hoggart corrects the "too-exclusively middle-class outlook" of the pioneers. Wondering what could be meant by "middle-class outlook" as applied to *Fiction and the Reading Public* (to which in *Culture and Environment* I referred the reader back), I find myself suggesting that the phrase *has* some point as applied to a left-wing intellectual journal that treated Mr.

Hoggart's predecessors in the way I record and the outlook of which on the literary side is fairly represented by the exaltation of Max Beerbohm into a major figure in contemporary letters, a fidelity to Norman Douglas (even — or especially — at D.H. Lawrence's expense), and Critic's comment, when Desmond MacCarthy was knighted, that it "ought to have been an O.M." At any rate, it seems to me (since sociology is in question) that there is matter for a profitable sociological inquiry here.

I am, sir,

Very sincerely yours,

F. R. LEAVIS

19. Lawrence's *"Existenz"*: The "Message" Versus the "Art"
To *The Times Literary Supplement*: April 5, 1957

Sir, — Middleton Murry adduced as illustrating Lawrence's "rooted
sadistic hatred" and his "adoption of a primitive mindlessness" (your
reviewer's phrases — I refer to the review of Murry's *Love, Freedom
and Society* in your issue for March 29) the passage about the West
African figure in chapter XIX of *Women in Love.* I pointed out that
Murry here (and very characteristically), through ignoring the nature
of that closely organized novel as a work of art, was guilty of a demonstrable and complete misrepresentation of Lawrence — a reversal of the
truth. I did this in the course of examining the "construction" (organization, I myself should prefer to call it) of *Women in Love,* for in
examining the "construction" I was — how could it be otherwise? —
examining the complexity of thought, attitude, and valuation (the
significance) that Lawrence's art was devoted to conveying. Your reviewer says that "it is to enjoyment of the style and construction of
particular works that Dr. Leavis calls us," and he seems to agree with
Murry at any rate to the extent of allowing that there may be some
better and surer way of arriving at Lawrence's essential communication.
("Enjoyment," is not the word that comes first — I, it's agreed, am still
"austere" — to me, but if we "enjoy" *Lear* and *Anna Karenina* the word
will do for *Women in Love.*) Murry himself, of course, could claim — he
made a point of claiming — to have known Lawrence personally (Lawrence had another view of the matter). Perhaps we are to take this as
constituting a conceivable advantage of Murry's as an authority on
Lawrence's *"Existenz"* (give me inverted commas as well as italics,
please) — a word which, when linked with "message", suggests that this
is some profound kind of significance beyond the purview of a mere
"enjoyer" of "style and construction." This possibility, however, only
confirms my strong feeling that *"Existenz"* is a term I would rather take
no risk of being supposed to be associating myself with.

Your reviewer suggests that there is some inconsistency between my
preoccupation with Lawrence as a great artist and my preoccupation with
him as "still the great writer of our own phase of civilisation" and concerned with the "questions and stresses" that are still ours. Clearly,
what is at issue is one's conception of art. Your reviewer's, whatever it
may be, is most certainly not mine. My own conception I took great
pains to make clear in my book on Lawrence. If I attach importance to
insisting that it shall not be misrepresented, I also — as everyone knows

— attach importance to Lawrence, and it is Lawrence's conception (a conception that is discussed as well as exemplified in *Women in Love*).

Is it a new or paradoxical conception? Is intelligent "enjoyment" of great art possible if one uses the terms "style" and "construction" — and "artist" — in the way favoured, it seems, by your reviewer? I have just (may I add? — I find it very relevant) been once more "enjoying the style and construction of particular works" of Aeschylus (the constituent parts of the *Oresteia,* in fact).

There is a dictum of Lawrence's (who, by the way, was much interested in Aeschylus) that seems to me to make a good close: "Art speech is the only speech."

I am, sir,
Very sincerely yours,
F. R. LEAVIS

20. Middleton Murry's "Knowledge" of Lawrence
To *The Times Literary Supplement*: April 19, 1957

Sir, — What moved me to write my letter to you a fortnight ago was
not, as your reviewer suggests it was, resentment at what I took to be a
gibe. I know what a gibe is: the fashionable gibe at me to which your reviewer refers was exemplified in the letter you printed in your issue for
April 5 and placed (by accident, no doubt) immediately after mine. A
radical misrepresentation that forms part of an elaborate argument is
another matter, and it was such I thought worth writing about. Your
reviewer now, in your issue for April 12, justifies me by persisting in
his misrepresentation — for it *is* a misrepresentation to associate me,
however insidiously, with a conception of art disowned by that which
my criticism actually invokes, implicitly and explicitly, and to suggest
that in the nature of things the critic is reduced to choosing between (to
me) unacceptable alternatives — or to mixing them incongruously: either
I treat Lawrence as Murry did, or I treat Lawrence's works as matters
for "mere enjoyment." "Mere enjoyment" is your reviewer's phrase; he
writes: "[Murry] resisted the mere enjoyment of works of art. He was
primarily concerned at once with the message of the work and the meaning of its author's life as a human destiny. This underlay his dispute
about D.H. Lawrence with Dr. F.R. Leavis, a dispute which is carried
further in the present book."

My criticism of Murry was, and is, that, refusing to read the work as
the highly organized work of art it is, he utterly falsified its meaning.
Women in Love (to stick to that example — it was written during the
war of 1914, the period of the alleged "adoption of primitive mindlessness") has *not* the advocacy of "primitive mindlessness" as its message,
or any part of its message. To affirm, as Murry did, that it has is to contradict what it says and is. Because in writing about Lawrence I insist
on this truth, and give my positive account of the significance that
Lawrence's art actually communicates when read as it asks to be read,
your reviewer remarks "how much neater and prettier the contrast
would have been if Dr. Leavis had contrived to have none of Murry's
preoccupations whatever." How much neater and prettier, that is, if I
had contrived to share the conception of art as a matter of "mere enjoyment." But in considering Lawrence's creative works I preoccupy myself with significance — significance in terms of basic human problems
and the fate of our civilization: *that* is the anomaly (for it is hardly
allegeable that I share any of Murry's particular ways of interpreting

62

Lawrence). To be consistent I ought to have left all that kind of preoccupation to Murry and confined myself to the "art", to "enjoyment
of the style and construction." Your reviewer cannot, he says, see the
point of my allusion to the *Oresteia*; I think it probable that some of
your readers have had no difficulty.

As for the "meaning of the author's life as a human destiny," if that
"meaning" is something to be arrived at by contradicting or ignoring
the meaning of Lawrence's creative works then it is certainly a preoccupation I myself don't share or favour. Murry, as I said, claimed as an
interpreter the special authority of one who had known Lawrence personally — personally or intimately (that was the insistent claim: he
opened his review of my own book by making it). My offence against
good taste was the suggestion that Murry knew as little of the real
Lawrence as he knew (to judge by his account of it) of *Women in Love*.
I was referring in the parenthesis constituting the offence, to Lawrence's
well-known insistences in the *Letters* that Murry's "love" and "faith"
regarded a Lawrence who didn't exist and had never existed. The burden
of many protests, ironies and disclaimers is what is summarized here, in
this passage from a letter dated May 20, 1929:

> "I don't understand you, your workings are beyond me. And you
> don't get me. You said in your review of my poems: "this is not
> life, life is not like that." And you have the same attitude to the
> real me. Life is not like that — *ergo,* there is no such animal. Hence
> my "don't care. . . ." And the me that you say you love is not me,
> but an idol of your own imagination. Believe me, you don't love
> me. The animal that I am you instinctively dislike — just as all the
> Lynds and Squires and Eliots and Goulds instinctively dislike
> it. . . . If I am the only man in your life, it is not because I am I,
> but merely because I provided the speck of dust on which you
> formed your crystal of an imaginary man. We don't know one
> another — if you knew *how* little we know one another."

I am, sir,
Very sincerely yours,
F. R. LEAVIS

21. Lawrence's *"Intelligibilia"*
To *The Times Literary Supplement*: May 3, 1957

Sir, — Your reviewer compels me to insist (so adding point, he will feel, to the delicate irony of his "compulsive") that it was not I, but he himself, who "chose the ground for this dispute." Whatever he may have thought he meant to mean — and his habit of expression, lending itself as it does to easy self-contradiction, gives him some excuse for uncertainty — those who look back at what he actually wrote in your issue for March 29 will see that it has no meaning except as proffering for acceptance this contrast between Murry's approach to Lawrence and mine: whereas Murry, "resisting the mere enjoyment of works of art," was concerned with significance, I, making "art" my distinctive pre-occupation, am concerned only with "enjoyment of the style and construction of particular works." Your reviewer offers to dispose of my right to protest by alleging some concession on his part that my "view of D. H. Lawrence is not a perfectly simple art-for-art's sake one." The concession is his original suggestion that I am inconsistent because I have after all written on "the questions and stresses of Lawrence as still the great writer of our phase of civilization" (it would have been better, I failed to see, if I had kept my view "perfectly simple.") And he now once again goes through what is essentially the same manoeuvre in slightly different terms: Dr. Leavis, he says:

> "started off as an evaluator and re-evaluator. This apparently makes it difficult for him to see that oneself may be concerned with *intelligibilia,* not with attitudes which may be adopted towards them."

Though this conveys nothing that can be called intelligible thought, it conveys a clear enough intention. It suggests that "evaluation" (my chosen line, we gather) has properly no direct concern with the thought, meaning, "message" and *"intelligibilia"* of the author's creative works, so that if I dispute an interpretation put on a work by Murry I am trying to do something quite out of my line and am disabled by my habits. It seems to me a notable sign of the times that a middle-page *Times Literary Supplement* reviewer should have permitted himself, and have been permitted, to fall back on insult when I repudiated the notion of "art" that is again proffered here.

The "evaluator's" and literary critic's concern with Lawrence's *"intelligibilia"* is more scrupulous, complete and disinterested than

64

LAWRENCE'S *INTELLIGIBILIA*

Murry's (who, "in fact", as your reviewer said, "barely considered Lawrence as an artist at all"). This position of mine is not an original or paradoxical one; it coincides with the position regarding art and thought held, and again and again expounded by Lawrence himself. Only by holding to it and insisting on it can one hope to arrive at Lawrence's *"intelligibilia"* and "message" or to defend him from misrepresentation. As for Murry, I have neither made any assault on him nor aimed at identifying your reviewer's position (whatever it may be) with his; I have merely defended Lawrence against the use of Murry as an authority against him, and I took *Women in Love* as my example because (as I said) it was written during the period of Lawrence's alleged "adoption of primitive mindlessness". The "treatment" to which I am objecting certainly "occurred a quarter of a century ago." But when Murry, not two years ago, reviewed my own book on Lawrence, though he found the explicit and argued challenge there, he made no retractation. And I note that your reviewer, in his original article, writes:

> "In the new book, Lawrence is shown adopting a primitive mind-lessness as a refuge from prostration by the First World War. . . ."

That insidious "shown" intimates very fairly the way in which the mischief is still working.

I am, sir,
Very sincerely yours,
F. R. LEAVIS

22. The Miltonism of Professor Tuve

To *The Times Literary Supplement*: September 19, 1958

Sir, – I too thought that Professor Rosemond Tuve's talk on Milton
(*The Listener,* August 28) invited comment, but the comment that
seemed to me above all called for is one that you do not make in your
commentary, *Idea and Image* (September 5). What I find significant
(and representative) in the talk is the way in which, in offering to place
with scholarly-critical authority – to place as superficial, fallacious and
now disposed of – the adverse criticism of Milton that has made him a
focus of discussion in the past two or three decades, Miss Tuve actually
paid that criticism no attention. If she really supposes herself justified
in suggesting that it amounts to nothing more than arbitrary and naive
ideas and demands in relation to Milton's "images" she can never have
paid it any attention. If she had ever made any serious effort to attend
to it she could hardly herself have been as naive about "images" as the
corrective critical enlightenment she offers the reader by way of arming
him against the anti-Miltonist shows her to be.

What I may for brevity call the post-Eliot case against Milton cannot
be reduced, as your article in summarizing Miss Tuve seems to suggest it
can, to a matter of Imagist ideas that we may think of as shared by the
"young Mr. Eliot" and the "young Mr. Pound." The whole Miltonic
habit as given in the Miltonic use of language is in question, as in any
intelligent discussion of his "imagery" it would have to be. This last
proposition involves a general truth about "imagery" and the intelligent
discussion of "imagery" as invited by any poet – a truth the force of
which seems to be very inadequately realized by Miss Tuve. "They
[Pound and Eliot] missed the point", you say in your commentary,
"which Miss Tuve makes, that Milton's language in *Paradise Lost* is
rhetorical in the traditional sense of being an artful language of persuasion, seeking to swing us to 'embrace or reject something': 'The
slightest element of metaphor brings into the images the factor of
directed evaluation.' " You do not here misrepresent the effect of Miss
Tuve's argument. So when you ask, "How then are we to read Milton?"
one's answer must be: "Not at any rate in the way to which Miss Tuve
(when we look for some positive upshot) seems to incite us."

I am not here taking up any such position as Miss Tuve represents by
Raleigh ("monument to dead ideas"); quite the contrary. It was characteristic of Raleigh's approach to literature that he should be able to
pronounce Shakespeare "morally neutral." I, on the other hand, was

recently described for your readers as a "Puritan critic." I didn't find
the elucidatory parallel with Calvin (a "great Puritan theologian") particularly enlightening, but your contributor's intention was clearly in part
flattering, and I supposed him to be constating an affinity between my
approach to literature and that of Lawrence (who, in the intellectual
world to which your contributor belongs, is, of course, also a Puritan).
Lawrence's account of why and how a creative work matters is one that
I would subscribe to. A creative work, when it is such as to challenge
and engage us to the full, conveys the artist's basic allegiances, his sense
of ultimates, his real beliefs, his completest sincerity, his profoundest
feeling and thought about man in relation to the universe. When I say
that a great work will inevitably have a profound moral significance I
am thinking of such a significance as will need to be described as religious, too.

Having notoriously the Puritan habit of approach I have indicated, I
have never favoured any treatment of *Paradise Lost* that reduces it,
Milton's theology being in question, to a "monument to dead ideas."
If I have come, as I see I have, to answering in terms of what I have myself written Miss Tuve's — and your own — suggestions about the nature
of the critical case that has been brought in our time against Milton, I
find my licence for the frank assumption of a representative status in
the way in which in the Sunday papers and the weeklies, and even in
foundation-lectures, I have figured as (malign influence being the criterion) the arch-anti-Miltonist. Do you, then (let me ask), endorse the
implication Miss Tuve unmistakably conveys when she speaks of a
"willingness to take Milton's theological theme seriously" as having
"entered" Milton criticism "in the second quarter of our century," so
constituting "an astonishing shift. . . in our ways of approaching the
study of images in *Paradise Lost*"? Miss Tuve clearly implies that it was
characteristic of the notorious adverse critics of Milton in that period to
refuse to take Milton's theological theme seriously; "taking seriously" is
defined by her references to Charles Williams and C. S. Lewis. It took,
we are to understand, the theological approach introduced by these
writers, the kind of "seriousness" *they* represent, to make the "shift"
out of a prevailing approach represented by Raleigh and (you yourself
contribute, quite congruously, this suggestion at any rate in its explicit
form) the Imagism of the "young Mr. Eliot" and the "young Mr.
Pound."

You seem to find nothing in Miss Tuve's talk that you cannot endorse. Yet you yourself, in approving the view that it is uncritical to

dismiss Milton's "theological theme" in Raleigh's way, say: "We may not be able to accept [Milton's ideas] literally as theological truth, but. . . ." What follows "but" would cover any approach that I myself should describe as taking Milton's theological theme seriously — taking it as it must, I have always assumed, be taken in intelligent appreciation of *Paradise Lost*. Miss Tuve, on the other hand, with her account of Milton's language as (I quote your article again) "rhetorical in the traditional sense of being an artful language of persuasion," seems to suggest, laying as she does all the stress on the "artful" kind of art, a strikingly naive conception of significance as it concerns the literary critic and of the interest of *Paradise Lost* as the creative work of a poetic genius. Milton is an interesting enough genius, *Paradise Lost* a challenging enough work, to impose on the reader who aims at an intelligent appreciation — of the poem, the "theological theme," the significance — a living realization of all that is implied in the now well-known Laurentian dictum: "Never trust the artist; trust the tale."

Miss Tuve's talk, I said, is representative — and so, I must add is your commentary. Mr. John Peter, writing in *Scrutiny* a half-dozen years ago (October, 1952) with some recent books about Milton in front of him, examined at length the habitual way in which the Miltonists — and the Miltonists command the academic world — virtually ignore the case that has been made against Milton (he refers especially to A. J. A. Waldock and myself), even while they make a show of discussing it. There prevails in the academic world, he observed (with illustrations), a tacit agreement either to ignore it altogether or to pretend that it is disposed of and needs no serious attention. What Mr. Peter noted holds true today. Book after book comes out, illustrating and confirming his observations and conclusions — one, addressed to the instruction of university students, came from Cambridge recently. Speaking as a university teacher, Mr. Peter deplores, with justice, the bad effect on students this policy of suppression and dishonesty must have; they "may easily conclude in self-defence," he says, "that the assessment of this poet is an improper activity."

I am, sir,
Very sincerely yours,
F. R. LEAVIS

23. Conrad's "Choice" of English
To *The Sewanee Review*: Autumn 1958

Sir, — Mr. Wain is either very casual or very cool. It is true that I had not for a very long time read through what I wrote about Conrad twenty years ago, and no doubt few readers of *The Sewanee Review* would have thought of checking Mr. Wain against the text of *The Great Tradition*. Anyone, however, who looks up what I actually wrote (page 17) will see that, if the words transcribed above[1] may be said to be mine, Mr. Wain must accept responsibility for more than the italics: the sense is his too — wholly his, since it contradicts mine. It is not so obvious a contribution as the italics, since he has effected it by excision. From the point at which Mr. Wain places his dots the words I wrote in *The Great Tradition* go on:

> . . .especially seeing he was so clearly a student of the French masters. And I remember the reply, to the effect that it wasn't at all surprising, since Conrad's work couldn't have been written in French. M. Chevrillon, with the authority of a perfect bilingual, went on to explain in terms of the characteristics of the two languages why it had to be English. Conrad's themes and interests demanded the concreteness and action — the dramatic energy — of English. We might go further and say that Conrad chose to write his novels in English for the reasons that led him to become a British Master Mariner.

In cutting out the three sentences that give André Chevrillon's reply Mr. Wain reverses the clear intention of the passage; for my whole purpose in bringing in the suggestion of a "choice" to write in English was that the suggestion might be repudiated ("Conrad's work couldn't have been written in French"). If Mr. Wain really thinks that the word "choose" in the piece of a sentence with which he closes his extract represents, as it stands in the unmutilated passage, a concession to the idea of "choice" that he himself advances (he thinks of a calculating choice determined by a favourable estimate of the British Public) — or

---

[1] Mr. Wain's quotation from *The Great Tradition* ran as follows: "I remember remarking to André Chevrillon *how surprising a choice it was on Conrad's part to write in English. . . Conrad chose to write his novels in English* for the reasons that led him to become a British Master Mariner." The italics were Mr. Wain's.

"choice" in any sense that is at odds with the judgment reported as M. Chevrillon's and plainly endorsed as my own — he is indeed a naive reader.

Finally, I would ask him to believe that Conrad's failure to find, in his life-time, an intelligent British public did, and does, seem to me a fact to be dwelt on and pondered (I need not insist on my reasons for referring to the symposium in *The London Magazine*).[1]

I am, sir,

Very sincerely yours,

F. R. LEAVIS

[1] Dr. Leavis's essay on Conrad's *The Shadow-Line,* which provoked Mr. Wain into writing a letter, is reprinted in *"Anna Karenina" and Other Essays* (Chatto and Windus, 1967).

24. The Wit of A. L. Rowse
To *The Spectator*: March 13, 1959

Sir, – I take due note of Mr. Rowse's piece of corrective information. I wrote in my article: 'a contribution the editor seems to have commissioned under a misapprehension, for Mr. Rowse never met Lawrence, and manifestly has no qualifications for saying anything enlightening of his own about him.' Instead of 'commissioned' I ought, I see, to have written 'included.'[1]

However, while the implicit criticism of the editor of the 'composite biography' was perhaps less severe than it now becomes, I cannot see that I did anyone an injustice. And we have now, I reflect, Mr. Rowse's wit to admire. These flashes of the brilliance of All Souls – further lights on a famed civilization – are worth having.

I am, sir,

Very sincerely yours,

F. R. LEAVIS

[1] Mr. Rowse had made a petty pother about the fact that his contribution to the Nehls 'composite biography' had not been specially commissioned by the editor. Dr. Leavis's review of *D.H. Lawrence: A Composite Biography* entitled "Romantic and Heretic?" is reprinted in *D.H. Lawrence*, (edited by H. Coombes), Penguin, 1973, pp. 393–397.

25. The Discrediting of Mr Grigson

To *Encounter*: June 1959

Sir, – Mr. Grigson, in the striking ethical demonstration you print in the April *Encounter* (that my attention should have been called to it will not surprise you) refers to *Commentary* as "well-known"; but if he had really supposed it to be well known in this country he could hardly have hoped that, by the method of decency and delicacy he demonstrates, it would be I who would be discredited rather than himself. *Commentary,* published in New York and addressed to a special American intellectual public, is in fact not at all widely known here, and few of your readers will have seen the article that Mr. Grigson adduces as justifying the treatment he favours me with. I had been asked by *Commentary* to make Mr. Eliot's last volume of critical essays an occasion for appraising his criticism in general, and anyone who reads my article will see that it is concerned with *that* – with the proposed examination and critique.[1] It contains nothing of the kind that Mr. Grigson imputes when he proposes that, as a fair retribution for the impertinences he accuses me of, writers like himself should practise their art in gratuitous publicities about my alleged private life. The postulate from which I start my critique is that Mr. Eliot is a major figure, not only as poet, but as critic: "that rare thing, a fine intelligence in literary criticism." That is, his work demands to be taken seriously, and to take it seriously is to enquire into its peculiar characteristics, its distinctive odd limitations and self-contradictions. One cannot do that without discussing the attitudes towards life, the habits of valuation, that are expressed in the documents and give them their significance. There is nothing in my article that does not refer to the published evidence strictly in this way, and come under this necessity.

Mr. Grigson intimates that it is patently absurd to judge that "Tradition and the Individual Talent", for all its authoritative note and its reputation is in an oddly significant way *not* a cogent piece of thinking. In being able to do this – and with such easy confidence – he confirms my view that radical enquiry into the nature of Mr. Eliot's achievement and influence as a critic was very much called for.

I am, sir,

Very sincerely yours,

F. R. LEAVIS

[1] The article, entitled "T. S. Eliot as Critic" was reprinted in *"Anna Karenina" and Other Essays* (Chatto and Windus, 1967).

26. Lawrence, Orwell, Amis and Leavis
To *The Times Literary Supplement*: December 11, 1959

Sir, – Whether the readers of your leading article "The English Gentleman" are meant to think of me as demonstratively lower-middle-class,
proclaimed such in my solemn "critical labours" by an ungentlemanly
"lack of reticence", or whether they are meant to think of me rather as
representing, in essential spirit, an Anglican "class-church" and a tradition of dominant English Good Form, I have not been able to make out.
The drift of suggestion seemed calculated to convey the former, till I
came to this:

> . . . Mr. Heppenstall's strictures. . . make the points that on histori-
> cal grounds the writ of the Church of England never ran through
> the whole kingdom and that this church in England is a "class-
> church." The bland way in which the English hegemony claims for
> itself, as part of the tradition, even those whom, like the Puritan
> Fathers, it drove into exile or, like John Bunyan, into prison is, in-
> deed, intolerable. We are probably not too far from the point where
> even D.H. Lawrence will become a respectable pillar of that tradi-
> tion and, when that does happen, Dr. Leavis will have to take a
> share of the blame.

What this means and how I am supposed to have incurred my guilt –
this remains obscure to me; but it doesn't, I think, much matter. What I
do feel called on to observe, prompted by the article as a whole (for the
level, at any rate, of the offered discussion is sufficiently plain), is that
my preoccupation in writing about Lawrence has always been to express
my sense of him as a great original genius – one of the greatest of creative writers and a supreme intelligence. I cannot myself see how such a
preoccupation, or such a sense, could consort with any tendency to discuss his significance in terms of the possibility of associating him in a
"norm" ("decent man" *versus* "gentleman" or any other such) with
George Orwell or Mr. Amis – or myself, whether I am to be thought of
as an "eccentric" (a polite formulation your writer uses) or (he seems
also to suggest) as the insidious agent of an English and Anglican
"hegemony."
   The point I make regards Lawrence. It does seem to me to matter,
and (oddly enough) to be called for.

I am, sir,

Very sincerely yours,

F. R. LEAVIS

27. The Degeneration of the Reading Public
To *The Guardian*: April 12, 1960

Sir, – One must expect to be surprised by one's Profile,[1] and, of the constituent notes embodied in that you print of me, I will ask leave to comment on only one – one that must seem to have been supplied directly by me, and the correction of which involves issues of general importance. The statement about translating German poems ("in the trenches") is not only something that I didn't, as a matter of fact, say; it obscures the theme I was intent on – and am. I had started by remarking how glad I was that the *Guardian* seemed inclined to give a more serious attention to literary criticism than in the past. The theme (which I insisted on ad nauseam, no doubt) was the change since 1914 in the situation facing anyone who thought that the state of literary criticism mattered. How different a public was assumed, I said by way of illustration, in the old "Saturday Westminster" from any that an editor could assume today! I was thinking of the competitions page (compare that in any contemporary weekly): Latin verse, Greek verse, niceties of French composition – and I remembered tackling a German war-poem that was set for translation (during the 1914 war!) in an issue sent out to me in France.

As the world changes, habits of thought can be dangerously slow to adjust themselves. The illustration I threw out may seem infelicitously emphatic: the cavalry massed behind the Somme, "ready for the break-through" with "miles of confluent shell-holes" in front. But the note of my "fanaticism" is just that I do think the menace frightening – that represented by the absence of any educated public large and coherent enough to support an intelligent literary review; for only in the interplay of thought and judgment in such a public can standards exist. And in this state of affairs the university and the university English school (this is part of my "fanatical" insistence) have a new function. Criticism, with all it stands for, is collaborative and creative. Mere lonely intransigence is barren.

These are the insistences I should have wished to be associated with in the "Guardian."

I am, sir,
Very sincerely yours,
F. R. LEAVIS

[1] The profile by John Bourne entitled "The Loneliness of the Long Distance Runner" appeared in *The Guardian* on April 8 1960.

28. The Radical Wing of Cambridge English
To *The Listener*: November 3, 1960

Sir, – My attention has been called to your attack on me in your leading article for October 20. 'Attack' is perhaps too complimentary a word, since it suggests a boldness of explicit and unequivocal criticism. Your actual method is one of insinuation – with minimal self-commitment. You confine all overt reference to me to this sentence – a crucial one for your purpose: 'It quickly becomes clear that Professor Lewis is really attacking the "radical" wing of Cambridge English, and that what we are witnessing is one more skirmish in the battle between "tradition" (the classics, "Q", the historical approach) and "nonconformity" (Dr. Leavis, psychology, sociology, and practical criticism)'.

What evidence you could adduce for interpreting Professor Lewis as intending an attack on me I cannot tell: I have not seen, and had not heard of, his article. *Delta,* however, was readily obtainable. I have looked through it, and I gather that the writers have arrived at a conclusion that corroborates yours. But what concerns me is your own attack on me; for you avowedly sympathize with that which you ascribe to Professor Lewis, and you implicitly offer yourself as speaking for an authoritative central body of the right-thinking and sane.

Your sense of the strength given you by this representative status would seem to have absolved you from any scruple about making clear just what charge you were bringing and what discussible argument you thought you were advancing: the ironic tone and the other familiar signals would draw the response you were counting on. And I, of course, cannot in the brief comment that alone is possible expose your insinuations for what they are, or deal with the misconceptions and misrepresentations they entail. I can only ask some questions, make some statements of position, and issue some challenges.

Will you, then, please explain what you mean by the 'non-conformity' that you appear to define in terms of me in association with psychology, sociology, and practical criticism? I do not think that your use of inverted commas absolves you from the need to justify yourself with something better than that parenthesis. You oppose 'nonconformity' to 'tradition', but I am prepared to give my grounds for contending that I, at least as much as any critic in our time, have stood for 'tradition' and the importance, for life and thought, of having a vital conception, and a robust and subtle sense, answering to that word.

'English as a *discipline*', you tell us, 'cannot be wholly divorced

from the historical past'. But what excuse have you for imputing to me
the suggestion that it can? (I find no such suggestion in *Delta* either.)
What distinguishes your own position, it seems to me, is a readiness to
rely upon empty phrases and inert preconceptions — which look like
something else to you because of your consciousness of enjoying massive
support. How does one get access to the 'historical past'? — that, surely,
is the great problem. But to you it is *no* problem: you see (it appears)
no relation between it and that delicate cultivation of perception, sensibility and intelligence which you refer to as 'practical criticism'.

You talk of exercises that 'have to be done correctly', and I suppose
you feel yourself qualified by having passed such tests. I note, however,
that, though you espouse one side in the 'battle' and identify the other
with me (for you mention no one else in the 'wing' that 'Professor Lewis
is really attacking', and I know of no ally you could have in mind), you
have felt no obligation to read what I have written, or, at any rate, to
pay attention to it: no scruple has prevented your being content with
the insinuations you find convenient. But I note too that you default in
this matter of 'correctness' in the most obvious and simple ways. For instance, you ask: 'who are the editors of *Delta*, who is any man, that they
or he should call Aristotle irrelevant?'

'Can the editors of *Delta*', I wondered, 'really have "dismissed this
dead mind"?' (The phrase is yours.) So I turned over the pages of *Delta*,
and found this: 'The *Poetics*, a work produced in one intellectual context, artificially applied to the completely different contexts of the
seventeenth and eighteenth centuries, is prescribed as a set book for an
introductory course in a modern discipline that can best be grasped
through the finest modern criticism, and say Johnson and Arnold, outstanding and *still relevant* critics of the past'. To refer to this view of
the *Poetics* as an insolent 'dismissal of Aristotle' seems to me to be an
unpardonable misrepresentation. To use the *Poetics* as it is used in
English courses is to treat not only the undergraduate and literary studies, but Aristotle himself, with the opposite of respect.

And I think you ought to tell us what we are to understand by your
irony about the 'canonization of George Eliot'. Do you mean that in
your judgment she is *not* a great writer? I have, in print, discussed also
Henry James, Conrad and D. H. Lawrence as great writers, and referred
to Jane Austen as one: is the undergraduate who thinks that such discussion of any of these is reasonable also 'assenting to a canonization'?
Must all novels be treated as *divertissements*?

My own conviction is that the work of the great English novelists constitutes one of the very greatest creative achievements of human history, that it should be studied by undergraduates reading English, and that such study entails a subtle initiation into thought about 'tradition'.

Let me end by saying that I think *Delta* right to insist that Cambridge undergraduates, in their studies, should be treated as adults — and that I (who have had no cognizance at all of the genesis or production of *Delta*) cannot see anything about that number that is not decent and intelligent. Professor Lewis himself, in launching such an attack, will hardly have expected to remain unanswered.

I am, sir,

Very sincerely yours,

F. R. LEAVIS

29. Mr Philip Toynbee as Latin Taggist and Critic
To *The Observer*: January 15, 1961

Sir, – Mr. Philip Toynbee believes that the "superiority of modern American poetry to our own" is due to America's happy immunity from my influence, which (we all know) does incalculable harm in this country. So much, at any rate, readers of his article in *The Observer* for January 8 will have been able to comprehend and carry away.

For Mr. Toynbee hasn't depended on his unsupported subtlety; he *names* me (not, after all, the more usual practice when his confrères of the embattled host, the co-defenders of criticism, English literature and the Humanities, demonstrate their disinterestedness and strike their opportune blows in that campaign). He too, no doubt, relies on a responsive solidarity in the *milieux* he is primarily addressing. Yet may not some readers have asked, and have not I a right to ask, what ground he can point to for offering to justify a disapproval of me with this?:

> My own inclination is to use a much-travelled quotation against –
> why not mention them? – Dr. Leavis and his proliferating disciples,
> *Nihil humanum mihi alienum puto.*

This formulation gets no added virtue from its context in what, being as polite as possible, one might call the succession of formulations, there being nothing in the article that can be called a sequence of thought. Mr. Toynbee was too preoccupied with establishing his own enlightenment and eliminating the possibility of reply to have any thinking left for logic or paraphrasable argument. He carefully demonstrates his mature adequacy to the difficult theme of Art and Morality. No one to-day, he tells us, can be an aesthete; no one can take the Tolstoyan moralistic line; and everyone can see that there must be some relation between the artist as man and the quality of his art. Mr. Toynbee himself sees it: his, we are to understand, is the central, the truly enlightened, position. What is there left for the sinister Influence (with his proliferating disciples) whom Mr. Toynbee, from his poised centrality, is placing? The Latin tag. The Latin gives a wise and judicial air to the insinuation.

The insinuation – for Mr. Toynbee himself has had to rely on insinuation, the stated charge would look too silly – could, if given an explicit meaning, only be that my criticism favours the kind of "moral" attitude that figured classically in the prosecution of "Madame Bovary." I notoriously, he implies, have shown that I need confronting with the truth he has made it his life's mission to vindicate and enforce: the principle that "everything which has been thought, felt, done or experienced by man should be accessible material for the poet or the novelist." This is his gloss on the Latin tag. He adds, however, italicising the phrase: "*without condemnation or praise*." "Hamlet," he tells us, "is the greatest work ever written in the English language." The judgment is a more arresting one than (to all appearances) he suspects, for he offers it in his modesty as an accepted commonplace. But more surprising still are the triumphant question and reply that follow: "And who is condemned or praised in that great work? Not even Claudius, surely?"

And that settles it: Shakespeare, like all great artists, is morally neutral; he merely *represents,* and there are no questions to be asked about implicit evaluative attitudes. Mr. Toynbee (though he takes the category "great" seriously, and seems to think he means something by calling "Hamlet" great) clearly thinks that he has said all that need be said about the relevance of moral sensibility to the appreciation of Shakespearean tragedy. It is almost incredible; there is a kind of sublimity about Mr. Toynbee's journalist-insouciance.

For he means his whole article to lead up, or to have the air of leading irresistibly up, to this conclusion, the formulation of the moral he himself draws from his reflections (it is to dispose of me and the proliferating disciples): "if we underestimate the extreme complexity and indirection of the relations between morality and literature we encourage a backhanded flippancy of judgment. . . . We over-estimate the literary merits of Lawrence."

This completes the placing of myself. I, the reader is to understand, have, with my well-known timidity or conventionality of moral, or moralistic, *parti pris,* my crude externality of approach, and my inability to appreciate the extreme complexity of the relations between morality and literature, committed myself to proclaiming Lawrence a great writer – an overvaluation the absurdity of which Mr. Toynbee could expose if he had time.

He is not as unequivocal about Pound as he is about "Hamlet" and Lawrence. But he pretty obviously means to be taken as concurring in the judgment that the Pisan Cantos constitute a "good poem", or at any rate as holding that the judgment is not absurd. Yet it is only convention that makes such an attitude seem safe to Mr. Toynbee – convention that owes its power to the authority of T.S. Eliot (who, in exalting the Cantos as a creative achievement, particularised that he wasn't interested in *what* Pound says, but in the way he says it)[1] and to the depressing, if not mysterious, fact that Pound is an accepted American institution, a major glory (the American Dante) of a major literature (the great world-Power being entitled to one). That few can believe they enjoy, few honestly profess to understand, the Cantos doesn't matter; they can be lectured on, researched on, expounded and appreciated — Eliot's authority has availed wonderfully in the establishing of an American classic.

Ph.D. research on the Cantos — we shall soon have it, if we haven't it already, in English universities. Mr. Toynbee may count on academic support. But to lend oneself to the humbug about Pound, while doing what one can to belittle the great creative writer of our time, that is what might with point, and just feeling, be called flippancy. And Mr. Toynbee's flippancy is not the less properly thought of as vicious because he has no more, in any serious sense of the word, *read* Lawrence (I think) than he has read the Cantos. (In what sense can he be said to have read "Hamlet"?)

I am, sir,

Very sincerely yours,

F. R. LEAVIS

[1] See also Letters 30 and 61.

30. The Ezra Pound Industry in England
To *The Observer*: January 29, 1961

Sir,— Mr. Toynbee's neat-footed mobility with his own polite weapon, the rapier, is such that my blunderbuss can avail nothing against him.[1] Making an urbane and kindly reference to my "proliferating disciples", he can drag me in for an insinuation meant, unmistakably, to be damaging, and when I reply and ask what charge he is intending to bring and on what grounds, I only illustrate on my own notorious bad manners. *Cet animal est très méchant.*

To Mr. Dekker[2] I must point out that, whether I am right or wrong about the Cantos, I expressed an adverse view of them when, bent on getting recognition for "Mauberley," I first wrote on Pound thirty years ago. There were then thirty of them, of which I was familiar with a good proportion before the book came out, having read them as they appeared in the old *Dial*. When, as an Editor of *Scrutiny*, I agreed to printing an essay[3] on them, and when, preparing "Determinations", I included that essay, the author of it knew that I disagreed with his estimate of the Cantos and deplored their influence on his own verse.

Mr. Toynbee (to do him justice) didn't invent his way of using the word "disciples" as a smear to discredit me and what I have stood for, but I confess that to me it seems a base and pitiful tactic, whether used by journalists or by the academic world that invented it in order to explain away "an awkward situation." Those I have worked with, in academic study and in critical enterprises, know that my adhesion to the truism that the life of criticism depends on an interplay of real, that is, personal, judgments is not merely theoretical. My "pupils" will see no paradox in the appearance in *Scrutiny* and *Determinations* of essays I didn't agree with. I thought — I urged — thirty years ago that Pound

---

[1] In his reply to Dr. Leavis's previous letter Mr. Toynbee wrote: "I suppose I should be flattered that Dr. Leavis hauled out so large a blunderbuss to fire at me. . . . One of the disciples recently explained his master's habitual ill-manners in controversy as a sign of his deep concern for literary values. . . . I daresay his one-time neglect had a bad effect on Dr. Leavis." And so on.

[2] Mr. Dekker pointed out that Dr. Leavis had included a sympathetic essay on the *Cantos* in his collection of essays by various authors, *Determinations*, (Chatto and Windus, 1934).

[3] By Ronald Bottrall.

was worth serious discussion, and did what I could to promote it. To hold that the Cantos now constitute a classical creative achievement, justifying a large and sustained academic industry of scholarship and exegesis, is another thing. And the "work on" Pound from America — the phrase-by-phrase analyses of the Cantos, the theses, the books — that has already come my way fully warrants my allusion to Dante. We shall do well not to take up that industry in this country — that is what I meant to convey. But if our escape depends on *my* influence in the Establishment, then, I assure Mr. Dekker, he needn't worry.

As for Mr. Toynbee, he too makes an extraordinary mistake in supposing (if he does) that *neglect* is what, over the past thirty years, I have had to complain of in the Sunday papers.

I am, sir,

Very sincerely yours,

F. R. LEAVIS

31. Mr. Alvarez as a Representative Intellectual Critic of Our Day

To *The Observer*: February 26, 1961

Sir, – "We must have mercy on critics who are obliged to make a figure in printed pages. They must by all means say striking things."

This remark of George Eliot's seems to me the kindest comment that can be made on the way in which Mr. Alvarez plunges into his article in today's *Observer* (February 19). He writes:

> "In 1932 Dr. Leavis announced that Eliot and Pound had, between them, re-orientated modern poetry, and he wrote a book to show what the "New Bearings" were.
> Twenty years later he took it all back again."

Mr. Alvarez must be referring to the Retrospect that I added to *New Bearings in English Poetry* in the New Edition (1950). I wrote:

> "And here, I suppose, I ought to admit a score against myself; for in speaking of the "re-orientation" as having made possible a modern English poetry I might reasonably have been supposed to entertain – as I did – not unhopeful expectations. Actually, I think the history of English poetry since then has been depressing in the extreme."

This is all that Mr. Alvarez can point to by way of justifying his brisk assertion that I "took it all back again." I did not in any respect "take back" what fills my book (which deals with Hopkins and Yeats as well as with Pound and Eliot) my account of the "New Bearings", the re-orientation. Such a change of assumption, judgment, preconceptions, taste and critical ideas has altered contemporary practice in verse-writing, contemporary criticism, and the general sense of the past of English poetry and its relation to the present. All I "took back" was my implicit too-sanguine anticipation of creative life to come. And the "history of English poetry since then", as I see it, has continued to be depressing. That, I think, can be largely explained by those conditions of our literary world and our contemporary culture which Mr. Alvarez, who is a representative intellectual critic of our day writing (one has to assume) for such effective cultivated public as we have, exemplifies.

I am, sir,

Very sincerely yours,

F. R. LEAVIS

32. The Trial of *Lady Chatterley's Lover*

To *The Spectator*: March 3, 1961

Sir, — If Mr. Martin Turnell wanted, by producing that obscure pioneer essay[1] (the printing was tiny, and the essay has been unobtainable for a quarter of a century), to show how bad a critic I was of Lawrence thirty years ago, he should have pointed to my unintelligence about *Women in Love*. That indeed is the significant thing about the passage he actually quotes[2], when it is read in its context. As I wrote a great deal later, disclaiming, in the course of controverting Middleton Murry's observations, all inclinations to 'superiority,' anyone who had tried, unguided (and there *was* no guidance), to find the right approach to so original a creative genius must certainly have found (if he continued to believe the trouble worth taking) that he had been unintelligent: by reason of one's habits of expectation, one hadn't been able to see what was there.

What I was certain of in 1930 (say) was that Lawrence was a great creative writer, though I knew there was a great deal I didn't understand in his work. What was important at that time — and for long afterwards — was to insist that he had a major claim on our attention, and above all, that he was not a pornographer, or anything of the kind. Now, thirty years later, things are very different. Work of critical advocacy has been carried on with some pertinacity — at the cost (I speak from painful experience) of obloquy, slander and worldly disadvantage ('The Leavis Prize for Pornography' was a permissible witticism in the Cambridge *Granta* in the 1930s: it was known to have been prompted at a senior level in the English School — 'Not that I don't like a good smoke-room story meself').

If I *had* been harsh to the defence witnesses Mr. Turnell's curious intervention might have been a little more intelligible.[3] But I was the reverse of harsh. Mr. Turnell does not dispute the justice of my general

---

[1]*D.H. Lawrence,* published as a pamphlet by the Minority Press, Cambridge, 1930. Part of the pamphlet has recently been reprinted in *D.H. Lawrence,* (edited by H. Coombes), Penguin, 1973, pp. 227—233.

[2]A passage from the pamphlet praising *Lady Chatterley's Lover.*

[3]Dr. Leavis is referring to his review of *The Trial of Lady Chatterley* edited by C.H. Rolph (Penguin Special, 1961). The review, entitled "The Orthodoxy of Enlightenment" can be found reprinted in *"Anna Karenina" And Other Essays* (Chatto and Windus, 1967).

account of the defence (*can* it be disputed?) and I confined myself to that. I was scrupulous to do no more, refusing the rich temptation to specify some of the absurd, conscienceless, evasive or irrelevant pieces of expert evidence. If he finds my tone objectionable, what does he think of the outrage on Lawrence (and decency) represented by Mr. C.H. Rolph's compèring, or of the spirit of self-congratulatory exaltation that is being displayed on all sides and is exemplified by (among other things) the advertised disc (the historic triumphant demonstration of enlightenment, rendered by actors and actresses, and recorded for posterity – and us)?[1]

Mr. Hetherington had already been informed by me why I could not accept the explanation he gives.[2] My letter to the *Guardian* was not about the Chatterley trial in general, but about his editorial. Since the *Guardian* doesn't reach me in time for breakfast, I wasn't able to read the editorial and write my comment on it before the evening. I posted it with my own hand the next day, and it ought (as I told him) to have reached his office the day after the first day on which any such letter *could* have arrived. And even if the post from Cambridge to Manchester is bad, I cannot see how Mr. Hetherington can pretend to expect that the explanation he offers will be accepted as good.

The editorial rebuking the Archbishop suggested (as if saying something obvious and unanswerable) that his objections against *Lady Chatterley's Lover* would apply equally to *Anna Karenina*, *The Scarlet Letter*, *Troilus and Cressida* and *Troilus and Criseyde*. I pointed out the gross and patent fallacy.

As I said in my article, I had not registered that Mr. Hetherington was one of the experts who gave evidence. I can't help now wondering how many of the others would have been moved to reject the astonishing assimilation.

I am, sir,
Very sincerely yours,
F. R. LEAVIS

[1] This was a recording of some of the previously omitted passages from *Lady Chatterley's Lover*.

[2] Mr. Hetherington claimed that he did not print Dr. Leavis's letter about *The Guardian's* editorial on the Chatterley case because it arrived too late. The editorial rebuked the Archbishop of Canterbury for his rebuke to the Bishop of Woolwich.

33. The Mummified Milton of Professor Kermode
To *The Spectator*: March 10, 1961

Sir, — In the *Spectator* for March 3 Professor Kermode writes: 'young
people are less prone to Donne-intoxication than they were twenty
years ago; it is also true that Milton and the Victorians are no longer
savagely excluded from their permitted reading.'

Where was Milton (where were the Victorians?) ever savagely excluded from permitted reading? At Professor Kermode's university? If so,
he ought to realise how abnormal — dangerously so for a critic and a
Professor of English Literature — his experience has been. If I challenge
his statement, however, it is because of implications it will certainly
have conveyed, and have seemed intended to convey, to most of the
readers of his article. No one who has looked through the recent book
of essays on Milton (*The Living Milton*) which he edited, and contributed
to, can fail to have assumed that he had me in mind, and meant his readers to have me in *their* minds, when he wrote the sentences I have
quoted. I can say this without laying myself open to charges of self-
importance, because I am explicitly named a good deal by his contribu-
tors as the arch-enemy, besides being (no one will question) made identi-
fiable as the malign pervasive Influence that the loyal members of the
team are faced with combating (the one member who is not loyal is for
that, very oddly, said by another, Mr. F.W. Bateson, to represent the
'Cambridge' point of view.)

The implications are: (1) that my criticism has for thirty years represented the official or dominant Cambridge English School, and dictated
the attitude of the dominant powers in the other English Schools; and
(2) that my criticism of Milton (or that common knowledge of me and
my character) justifies the assertion that I, by savage means or otherwise, would have eliminated Milton from the student's reading if I had
been able.

Implication (1) it is my duty, in justice to my own university, to
rebut by invoking the brute and verifiable facts. When, then, my earlier and forgivable essay on Milton appeared, I, though forty, had been
without a salaried post for some years — and I continued so for more.
This was generally understood to be because my influence, if I should
be allowed to have any, would most certainly (it was felt) be bad. If
Professor Kermode puts someone on to doing a little research in the
weeklies and the Sunday papers from 1930 till when Desmond Mac-
Carthy reviewed Mr. Eliot's famous British Academy lecture (making

his review an attack on me), he will be able to have it established that both the Cambridge attitude and his own were consistently endorsed by the literary world. That is, there is not the slightest excuse for suggesting that there was ever a dominant anti-Milton orthodoxy. And Cambridge 'English' must be held altogether absolved.

Implication (2), in which Professor Kermode is conscious of having an immensely larger body than his team with him, makes me despair, so dominant is the basic hostility to any free play of critical thought that it portends. I do not ask that he should have *read* my criticism – read it for what it says. Without that he could have known, if he had wanted to, what would (I hope) have shamed him out of the impulse to indulge in that slanderous implication. All pupils of mine know that I have always been very far from discouraging the reading of Milton, and that when, twenty years ago, I defended Milton against an eminent Miltonist, my title was not merely ironical. I have always held that Milton is a very great power, and that without an intelligent study of him one cannot understand English literary history. If one is not intelligent about him, I think it improbable that one will be intelligent about Donne (and certainly that one cannot be intelligent about Eliot). But, if we are to talk about what is, and what is not, permissible, the fact I have to state is that students likely to be thought of as pupils of mine ('disciples' – 'Leavisites') have long been afraid to answer on Milton in the examination room. It is the Mummified Milton that such an academic world is bent on preserving.

And to Professor Kermode I would suggest that it is not noble, when you are bent on perpetuating an orthodoxy that has long been in possession, to point to the heretic who has survived, somehow, as the Establishment you are bravely displacing. Professor Kermode can of course reply that *that* is just what is being done by the best people, and not merely in respect of Milton.

I am, sir,

Very sincerely yours,

F. R. LEAVIS

34. The Jocular Ways of Professor Kermode
To *The Spectator*: March 31, 1961

Sir, – When Professor Kermode was making, in his jocular way, the point (to quote the rendering we are now given) that 'many young people were encouraged, prematurely, to undervalue Milton and compare him unfavourably with Donne,' it didn't occur to him that his readers might think he had me in mind as an arch-encourager. Mr. Dyson, writing to corroborate this affirmed innocence, relates that when, in 1945, he was preparing for a Cambridge scholarship, he was warned against 'parading a taste for Milton and Tennyson': advice, he modestly hazards, that was 'not unusual at that time.' Where his adviser's 'views on Milton came from,' Mr. Dyson goes on, 'is anybody's guess,' and proceeds immediately to suggest what anybody's guess might be:

> "Perhaps he had read in *Revaluation* that 'Milton's dislodgment in the last decade, after his two centuries of predominance, was effected with remarkably little fuss,' and arranged his own permitted reading accordingly."

The advantage of the insinuation-technique is that it enables you to protest your innocence. If I say that Mr. Dyson's subsequent introduction of the names of Eliot and Middleton Murry doesn't make the sentence I have quoted any less an example of the technique, I confirm the well-known diagnosis of persecution-mania (as I do when I say that a Part-Time Lecturer of very junior standing cannot reasonably be adduced as representing a menacing Cambridge orthodoxy of 1945). Nevertheless, I assure Professor Kermode and Mr. Dyson that when I take them up it is not merely self-defence I am engaged in: impersonal issues of very great moment are my main concern (and if one is not a living individual, and in a particular situation, one cannot have an impersonal concern).

Mr. Dyson, then, with that 'arranged his own permitted reading accordingly', lends himself unmistakably to the insinuation Professor Kermode's innocence of which he is offering to endorse. Professor Kermode, in the letter printed just above Mr. Dyson's, himself brings out the insinuation once again: he assumes without the least excuse – the assuming amounts to asserting as known fact ('It *is* so; we all *know* it is') – that when I required Professor Ford to read Milton I was really exacting from him a meek docility and instructing him to be sure that,

88

whatever laborious show of reading he might go through, he came
away with the opinions I had required him to learn and subscribe to.

What makes me (as I said in my first letter) despair is that Professor
Kermode, with an obvious sense of being strongly supported, should
wish to have that believed of me — should wish to make intelligent discussion of Milton impossible. He promotes, in this, a spirit of general
hostility to the free play of critical thought. Any pupils of mine if I
had behaved about Milton in the way he insinuates (jocularly this time
too?) would have been able to reflect with ironical amusement, that at
any rate they had been assiduously trained to place and despise that
kind of aberration. You cannot be intelligent about literature without
judging. A judgment is a personal judgment or it is nothing — you cannot have your judging done for you. The essential form of a judgment
is 'This is so, isn't it?', and the question (it is a real request for confirmation) expects, at best, a reply of the form 'Yes, but. . .' Here,
diagrammatically (so to speak), we have given us that collaborative
process by which valuations are established as something 'out there'
about which we can profitably discuss our agreements and disagreements.
Pupils of mine will testify that immeasurably more of our time together
in any year is taken up with my offers to enforce, one way or another,
directly and indirectly, these truths than is given by me or them to
Milton (or Donne). And it is a further truism (they are very familiar
with it as such) that only by the collaborative-creative process I have
alluded to can a living literary culture — and all that goes with it — be
created and maintained.

My excuse for this reminder of fundamentals is that Professor
Kermode and Mr. Dyson make it necessary. Their line is to make the
collaborative process impossible.

I may be wrong about Milton, but I have never expressed the views
or attitudes they ascribe to me: the process they collaborate in is that
of identifying me with propositions that absolve them (they feel) from
having to answer what I have really (and very carefully) written. Both
lower themselves to that familiar play with the word 'dislodgment';
Professor Kermode goes so far as to write (jocularly?) of my 'plans for
the "demolition" and "dislodgment" of Milton.' Where he found the
word 'demolition,' which with flagrant intention he puts in inverted
commas along with 'dislodgment,' I don't know, but he has no excuse
at all (nor has Mr. Dyson) for pretending that an intelligent and disinterested reader could take 'dislodgment' in that way. There had been
recently made manifest a decisive change (closely bound up with the

recognition of Eliot) in taste, assumption, critical ideas and poetic practice. In these, for two centuries, Milton had been prepotent (and what I
mean by this contention I have explained with very great care in a later
essay)[1] an aspect of the change was that Milton lost this prepotence —
he was 'dislodged' from it. It is possible to hold this view while continuing to believe that Milton is a great poet. It is not, I think, possible,
while refusing to consider such a view discussible, to be intelligent about
Eliot's achievement or the distinctive poetic life of our time.

Why have Professor Kermode and his ally steadily refused to do anything in reply to these contentions but misrepresent them and attempt
to dispose of them by insinuations against the contender? When I used
the word 'dislodgment' I was being what I imagine Mr. Dyson means by
'hard-hitting.' That is, I believe that one should be clear with oneself
about one's judgments, and state them as clearly, responsibly and
challengingly as possible: one will then have exposed oneself unequivocally, and the process of correction will have been facilitated. Insinuation is a different thing.

Milton is a large and immensely significant fact: you cannot repress
the life of critical thought *here* without inflicting general damage —
whether you want to or not. And you cannot be really a promoter of
life anywhere if you promote, or connive at, such repressions. I say
this sadly, for I believe that the English Schools of our universities have
a very important function.

I am, sir,
Very sincerely yours,
F. R. LEAVIS

[1] "Mr Eliot and Milton" in *The Common Pursuit* (Chatto and Windus, 1952).
The earlier essays on Milton which Dr. Leavis refers to are in *Revaluation*,
(Chatto and Windus, 1936) and *The Common Pursuit*.

35. Parody

To *The Spectator*: January 5, 1962

Sir, – Mr. Julian Jebb wonders in the *Spectator* why, in my concern to promote the intelligent study of literature, I haven't recommended the writing of parody, so perhaps I may be allowed some not very original observations (they seem to me truisms).

There is only one thing that could be learnt by the attempt to parody a writer whose distinction makes him worth close study; that is, how inaccessible to any but the most superficial, and falsifying, imitation the truly characteristic effects of such writers are. Mr. Julian Jebb speaks of 'the greatest parodies.' He illuminates the significance of that category by instancing Mr. Connolly's parody of Aldous Huxley and Mr. Kingsmill's of *The Shropshire Lad.* No one will be much disturbed by Mr. Connolly's or Mr. Kingsmill's parodying Mr. Huxley or Housman, and no one called on to make the essential critical points about the novelist and the poet would (I postulate an intelligent interest in literature) think parody an intelligent or profitable way.

Why not offer a 'great parody' of Shakespeare? We all know why. What does the parody of Wordsworth in *Rejected Addresses* tell us about the great Wordsworth? Nothing. The parodist may practise his art upon (say) G.K. Chesterton or even Macaulay, without moving anyone to indignation. But there have been literary connoisseurs who thought they could parody Johnson; and to offer to parody Johnson is to expose oneself. Worse, it is to further that cult of Johnson which precludes – which is inevitably and essentially hostile to -- the recognition of Johnson's greatness.

The cult of parody, in fact, belongs to that literary culture (a predominant one, to judge by our intellectual weeklies – it is a branch of 'social civilization') which, in its obtuse and smug complacency, is always the worst enemy of creative genius and vital originality. It goes with the absurd and significant cult of Max Beerbohm – whom (to make, with one illustration, one directly relevant point) it is impossible to forgive for his kindly parody of poor James; a parody which did all it could to identify James with the complacently stupid preconceptions of that literary world which – to his death – denied him all intelligent recognition. Conrad, too, suffered from Beerbohm's attentions.

People who are really interested in creative originality regard the parodist's game with distaste and contempt.

Mr. Jebb needn't feel that he has been insulted in any way he need

PARODY

worry about: 'Write a criticism of Pope in the style of Pope' – that
invitation, or one substantially to the same effect, I remember to have
seen in an English Tripos paper.

I am, sir,

Very sincerely yours,

F. R. LEAVIS

36. Classical Education and Parody
To *The Spectator*: January 26, 1962

Sir, – I have to thank Mr. Mark Mortimer[1] for making about the classical education the point I refrained from making explicitly in my own letter: that it explains the persistent power (even in intellectual organs of the Left) of the literary culture that fosters parody and the cult of Max Beerbohm.

I am, sir,
Very sincerely yours,
F. R. LEAVIS

[1] Mr. Mortimer pointed out in a letter that students of Greek and Latin literature have at least to imitate the authors they study, if they do not actually go as far as to parody them.

37. Joan Bennett on the Cambridge English School

To *The Times Literary Supplement*: April 20, 1962

Sir, — As Mrs. Bennett has recently pointed out in your columns, the Cambridge English School ought not to be exposed to the suggestion that I am its voice, or that my work represents the school's ethos and influence.[1] If, then, I reply to the suggestion you print from Mr. B.M.G. Reardon regarding Mr. R.H. Stringer's letter, it is as one who merely happens to know the relevant fact: Mr. Stringer did not take the English Tripos. The style of the letter cannot, therefore, fairly be laid either to the discredit or to the credit of the Cambridge English School. By him, certainly, the school could be in no way compromised.

I am, sir,

Very sincerely yours,

F. R. LEAVIS

[1] Mrs. Bennett wrote to the *TLS*: ". . . You write as though Dr. Leavis speaks for the 'English School at Cambridge.' This is, of course, not so. The school has a rich diversity of teachers. . . . they could not be represented by any one man, least of all, perhaps, by one with so personal a voice as Dr. F. R. Leavis." Mr. Reardon made a sarcastic remark about the prose style of Mr. Stringer's letter and suggested that it might be an example of the style of the Cambridge English School.

38. Greek Tragedy and Hellenists
To *The Times Literary Supplement*: December 28, 1962

Sir, — In your front-page article "How Good is Tasso?" I read this:
"The Greek and Latin classics have been silently dropped as a topic of
literary conversation. To refer to an ancient author is a little presump-
tuous, if not suspect — has not Dr. Leavis warned us that, if we do not
see how impossible it is to read Aeschylus as we read Shakespeare, then
we cannot really read Shakespeare?"

This I suppose will have been taken by your readers to be irony at
my expense, but what is meant to be the force of the irony? Does your
contributor suppose that one *could,* if one's Greek were good enough,
read Aeschylus as one reads Shakespeare? Hardly. Does he then mean
to imply with his "warned" that when I invoke the truism my aim is to
eliminate Aeschylus from the necessary reading of the educated man, or
to discourage the study of the Greek tragic writers?

If so, for all his air and tone, he knows little about me and my habit
as one whose business it is to promote the study of literature. My
"warning" is a reminder of the hard work that must be done, and the
strenuous modesty of judgment and interpretation that must be cultivated, if one's approach to what most certainly can repay the approaching is to bear its profit. For I do not myself think Aeschylus "inaccessible" — the word used by a recent critic in one of the intellectual weeklies. But I do think that anyone who supposes him to be not more
essentially difficult of access than Shakespeare doesn't know what
literature (or a language) is. When I utter the "warning" it is as one who
is notorious for insisting that no candidate for Part II of the English
Tripos should be allowed to suppose that he will pass as having done
creditably in the Tragedy paper if he has not worked hard to make
himself intelligent about Greek tragedy.

For taking this line, and divulging that "English" as I endeavour to
foster it entails a great deal of "conversation" about Greek tragedy, I
have been snubbed by Hellenists who think that only professional
Hellenists can decently discuss the Greek tragic writers. But after all
I am suspected of suspecting that there have been distinguished classical scholars who could not read Shakespeare — or Jane Austen.

I am, sir,

Very sincerely yours,

F. R. LEAVIS

39. The Challenge of Dickens
To *The Spectator*: January 4, 1963

Sir, — Mr. Peter Fison opens a review in your last week's issue by telling your readers that "Dr. Leavis, of course, doesn't like Dickens." What information Mr. Fison is relying on I can't guess. Or perhaps (and the 'of course' may imply it) he relies on his unaided intuition. In any case, as some of your readers (I think) could tell him, his trust is misplaced. If he enquires around, or even reads what I have written, he will find that for a number of years, one of my main preoccupations in writing and speech, has been the "challenge of Dickens" — the challenge he presents to criticism to define the ways in which he is one of the greatest of creative writers.

I will say here, what I have found myself saying in discussion, that (if one can imagine oneself faced with such a choice) I would without hesitation surrender the whole *oeuvre* of Flaubert for *Dombey and Son* or *Little Dorrit*. This, however, may confirm Mr. Fison's view of me (and he can tell himself that he has Dame Edith Sitwell with him) as a comic character. I will nevertheless add that to lay the kind of emphasis Mr. Fison does upon *The Old Curiosity Shop* seems to me a poor tribute to Dickens's genius, and that to talk of "folk tradition" by way of 'appreciating' the business of Little Nell and her grandfather advances neither the recognition of that genius nor the usefulness of 'folk' as a critical term.

Dickens in learning how to become a novelist and developing out of a journalist and a popular entertainer into a great artist, became more and more conscious of himself as such. Like all great writers a great technical innovator, he created a highly subtle, penetrating and sophisticated art — an art that made him an incalculably potent influence in the work of his greatest successors.

I am, sir,

Very sincerely yours,

F. R. LEAVIS

40. The Banning of *Ulysses*
To *The Times Literary Supplement*: May 3, 1963

Sir, — There weren't, as far as I know, more persons than one charged, "round about 1925", with intending to lecture at Cambridge on *Ulysses,* so I think the young graduate of the affair that is referred to by Mr. Reginald Horrox in the letter ("Freedom to Read") you print from him in your issue for April 19 must have been myself. Actually there was more fuss than Mr. Horrox suggests, for the total fuss was of a kind that doesn't make itself felt as fuss — except (in due course) by the offender. Mr. Horrox could hardly have known of it. Nor could he very well have had a clear view of the immediate facts, which weren't quite as he states them. His letter leads me to think that there may be some point in my giving in brief the actual history: the changes in our civilization at which he glances are of some general interest.

One day a conversation with my bookseller about the censorship exercised by the American Customs led to my saying: "Well, *we* can't talk: there are books you can't get me." The upshot was that, at his suggestion, I dictated a letter to the Home Office requesting permission to import a copy of *Ulysses,* by James Joyce, for use by me at Cambridge in a course of lectures on English prose — I was down on the lecture-list for such a course.

A week or two later I received an invitation to call on the Vice-Chancellor. When, at the appointed hour, I introduced myself to him in the Master's Lodge at Downing (a college with which I then had no connexion), he handed me a typescript several pages long from the Public Prosecutor. This contained an account of me and my lectures (number of undergraduates attending, proportion of women, &c.), the product of investigations carried out by the Cambridge police. It contained also an account of the book ("indescribably filthy", &c.: "We do not suppose you have read it, and shall be pleased to send you a copy for examination"). It closed with the expression of an undoubting confidence that I should be suitably and firmly dealt with. In fact, I couldn't help believing that Sir William Joynson-Hicks himself[1] had drafted this descriptive and hortatory part of the document, and sent it round for

---

[1] Sir William Joynson-Hicks, widely known as 'Jix', was Home Secretary at the time of the anti-obscenity proceedings against D. H. Lawrence in the late nineteen-twenties.

the Public Prosecutor's use.

I told the Vice-Chancellor (Professor Seward) the facts about my application; said I had never entertained the absurd idea attributed to me by the Public Prosecutor – that of prescribing *Ulysses* for study for the English Tripos; remarked that I didn't see why anyone who wanted to read the book, which everyone interested in contemporary literature was expected to be able to discuss intelligently, shouldn't be free to read it – or to try, and that it was in any case widely current among Cambridge undergraduates: "I happen to know", I said, "that there are copies circulating at both Girton and Newnham." What I should have liked to eliminate, I added, was the glamour of the clandestine attending the cult – for there *was* a cult. "I could easily have got a copy", I said, "by letting myself be put in touch with one of the disreputable agents every bookseller knows of." "I'm glad you didn't do that", the Vice-Chancellor replied; "letters get intercepted." And he touched with an admonitory finger one of the pigeon-holes of the desk at which he was sitting. He didn't seem at all disturbed, and I think he replied to the Public Prosecutor in the terms of my explanation.

I heard nothing of any further official action, and (though not granted a licence to import *Ulysses*) used, and went on using, a passage of Joyce's prose in my lecture-course. A "fuss", however, not the less potent for being of a muted kind, inevitably got a start – and developed, for the Vice-Chancellor had inevitably made inquiries that were passed on to the *de facto* centre of power in the English School. To say that harm undoubtedly resulted for me isn't primarily to indict anyone, though naturally I could make – and substantiate – some severe judgments. The moral I have in mind regards the potency of convention, and the way in which convention has changed. It was very natural at the time of Lawrence's death, and later, for ordinary conventional academics to say, with an untroubled conscience, when asked how Leavis had earned so marked a disfavour: "We don't like the kind of book he lends undergraduates." After the notorious scandal, to have gone on (in the *Cambridge Review*!) to D. H. Lawrence and T. F. Powys – it was, in those days, asking for it. For those were days when the non-academic librarian of the English Faculty Library was able, with the sanction of the academic Faculty Librarian, to withhold D. H. Lawrence's and T. F. Powys's books from undergraduates who wanted to borrow them, or read them in the library.

Convention has made so complete a change since then that it is possible for those who aim at discrediting this recall of a not distant past to feel that "persecution-mania!" will do all that is necessary. Yet there is abundance of evidence that is not difficult of access. The point I want to emphasize is that the very people who find "persecution-mania" a sufficient comment are quite likely to have been heard, a short while ago, testifying in court that they thought it would be a good thing, and tend to strengthen the respect for marriage, if *Lady Chatterley's Lover* were on sale, cheap, in every Woolworth's in the country.

I will end by saying that the upshot (as I see it) of these historical notes is that "Freedom to Read" doesn't seem to me to make the right emphasis. It doesn't point to the essential issue. For that there *is* an issue at stake of great moment for our civilization I am deeply convinced.

I am, sir,
Very sincerely yours,
F. R. LEAVIS

41. The Organic Community

To *The Spectator*: May 10, 1963

Sir, – Maureen O'Connor writes (*Spectator*, May 3): 'Yet, being objective, one has to admit that the origins of pub atmosphere are lost in the roseate prehistory charted by Dr. Leavis.'

Will Miss O'Connor, being objective, tell your readers when I did this charting, and where they can find it? If I read the passage with surprise, that was not because the phenomenon exemplified was new to me, but because it had assumed in her article so blithely reckless a form. I will venture that she couldn't say where in anything written by me she thinks she could find plausible warrant for her allusive and insinuating irony. It is gratuitous and routine – a matter of common form: she gets the confidence for it from the habit or 'culture' (to use Sir Charles Snow's word), of that literary world which fosters its morale in the *Listener,* the intellectual weeklies and the Sunday papers.

She should be adverted, then, that a habit of sneering allusion, even when established in such force, doesn't suffice to establish the alleged fact. Twenty authorities of the order of *Lucky Jim* wouldn't, the given kind of smear being in question, justify the confidence with which she lends herself to it. And she should note that, when reviewers commit themselves to bringing in my name (as Mr. Amis, in that book does not) they prefer to be less explicit in allegation than she is. Their boldness takes no greater risks than those braved by that notorious colleague of mine who illustrates his gift of discreet irony in genial by-references to 'the old wheelwright's shop.' Everyone knows who it is he has in mind, and what kind of general smear he intends. Since it entails no mention of my name, and the generality is so indeterminate, he needn't worry about the possibility of being answered.

His ironic formula, however, gives me an opportunity to inform her of an immediately relevant fact: my colleague is pointing to the only show of excuse that could be alleged for the fabrication she offers to reinforce. George Sturt's *The Wheelwright's Shop* is (along with many other books) referred to in *Culture and Environment,* which came out thirty years ago and has been used in schools ever since. Miss O'Connor can easily get hold of a copy and establish for herself how different in spirit and purpose it is from what my colleague's sarcasms would impute. *The Wheelwright's Shop* forms part of the documentation adduced to bring home the truth that there was once an organic community. It is a truth and not something invented by me. Miss O'Connor could find historians and sociologists enough who would assure her that it is a commonplace. And the sneer she takes up — that expresses merely the confidence of ignorance: the characteristic ignorance of the 'literary intellectual.' No one truly interested in the conditions that produced our literature, and truly concerned for its life, could countenance the sneer or the ethos.

To insist on the need to promote a common awareness of the nature of the immense changes being brought about in our civilization, and of the danger of an unconscious acquiescence in the human impoverishment that may, unrecognised as such, attend automatically on a technological progress towards a civilization of 'more jam' is not to indulge in, or to promote, or in any way to favour, romancing about the past.

Miss O'Connor may have been led to suppose, of course, that she could find her justification in my Richmond Lecture, *Two Cultures?* If she reads it — it is accessible in book form (perhaps I may say, since it virtually escaped being reviewed) — she will discover how utterly unfounded and at odds with the actuality that idea is.

I am, sir,

Very sincerely yours,

F. R. LEAVIS

42. The Transition from Quality to Quantity in Education
To *The Times Literary Supplement*: August 9, 1963

Sir, — If a concern for a serious standard is a "nostalgic reminder",
then Dr. Bradbrook and Dr. Hough are at liberty to apply that adjective
to me. What has to be fought for is certainly in worse danger than it
was thirty years ago, and, weighing my words, I am willing to be placed
on record as having said that if we don't fight with at least some measure
of success there will have been a grave defeat for civilization. It is not
paradox, I imagine, that they will charge me with if I say that in our
day, when academics make and consolidate reputations as intellectuals
on the radio and in the Sunday papers, the standards that we non-
scientists have it as our business to care for suffer constant assault,
overt and insidious. "Doesn't he know he's selling the pass?" it was
asked recently with reference to a public utterance by a senior member
of my university who is thought to have an influential voice in the field
of education. "He doesn't know there is a pass to sell", came the reply
from a younger member of his college.

It is absurd of Dr. Bradbrook and Dr. Hough to turn any irony they
may have detected in my article into a "sneer at Africa and the Common
wealth". The irony applies to those who should utter nobly about
"transmitting the incomparable wisdom for living that English literature
can supply" while actually promoting changes that would make talk
about such "transmission" a mockery. What they implicitly avow is
their irresponsibility: they don't deny that the innovations they have
been contriving entail a surrender of standards; they don't dispute my
evidence that some of the students admitted to research in recent years
couldn't have hoped to take the English Tripos with much credit; but
when asked, "What, then, do you propose to do to safeguard the position and the rights of the traditional kind of research-student?", they
answer, if at all, with a shrug. Their attitude towards their work of destruction is to be bland and blank. The old kind of research-student —
with (one interjects) a great deal else that belonged with him — is
superseded; to worry about that is to be nostalgic. We now have to deal
with the vast regions of the world and with numbers; we must make the
transition from quality to quantity.

It doesn't perhaps sound so gross, the betrayal doesn't immediately
seem so flagrant, when they talk of our responsibility towards Africa
and the Commonwealth. But when, with an unconsciousness that
plainly signifies an habitual not-thinking, they go on to tell us that the

"demands of the new universities in this country cannot be ignored", who will not come out with the reply: the first and inalienable responsibility of Oxford and Cambridge is to maintain the standard? Their doing that is the condition of any real help they may be able to give the new universities. To default in that responsibility on the plea of meeting the "demands" of the modern world, or any demands, is to play into those processes of our civilization which it is preeminently the function of the universities in general to resist.

I speak of the humane function. In respect of the sciences there is not the same problem; for reasons I need not go into, there is no equivalent desperate defence of standards necessary and the nature of standards is unequivocal. But the fact that in our field they are not in the same way producible and don't lend themselves to demonstration doesn't make them the less real and essential. If they are not somewhere maintained, work everywhere is disabled and the whole community is let down.

I have never met with any slowness to appreciate these truths among the research-students from the new universities whom I have had to do with. They came to Cambridge because of the high standard they believed to be maintained there, with the intimately associated possibility of pursuing, unhampered and undiscouraged, an intelligent study of literature. Dr. Ian Jack will take it as confirming his view as to my parochialism when I add that that's why they chose Cambridge rather than Oxford. But he is mistaken in supposing me to contend that only persons who have taken the English Tripos should be considered fit to research in English at Cambridge. One of the advantages of offering the conditions that are inevitably desired by genuine research students is that the university gains by attracting an elite. I say this with a warm sense of gratitude: I number students from the Commonwealth, the United States, the Scottish universities and the new universities among those I know as having notably justified their presence at Cambridge. Such students, when they go, immensely strengthen the wider community on which our hopes in the battle I have referred to must depend.

I feel justified in ignoring Dr. Jack's observations about research and my parochialisms since he, it seems to me, ignores my postulate: research in "English" – what it should be and what place it should have – cannot be profitably discussed except in relation to the nature and place of "English" as a whole in the university. And here I can with immediate relevance say that Mr. S.J.R. Noel seems to me to describe admirably the way in which a "research" undertaking in English should be thought of.[1] I hadn't intended to be understood as advocating anything different. Nor do I think that Mr. Philip Hobsbaum and I disagree as seriously as he imagines. When I said that a research student should be a first-class man I meant — and meant consciously — that he should be the kind of man who *ought* to get a first in the Tripos. But I was troubled enough by my sense of the complexity of the essential argument that had to be presented, and in so brief a space; the question of the unsatisfactoriness of the traditional Tripos examination had better not, I thought, be explicitly brought in. Let me, however, assure Mr. Hobsbaum that a high proportion of the first-class men I have known — men preeminently qualified to be recruited as of the kind needed if an English school is to be kept in touch with what I have referred to as the "creative front" — were not placed in the first class in the Tripos list. It is my conviction (strong grounds for which will, I think, occur to Mr. Hobsbaum himself) that the misleadingness of the Class List showing would become decidedly worse if innovation in the spirit represented by Doctors Bradbrook, Hough and Jack were to be consummated. You cannot compromise standards in one part of the School in that way without general deleterious consequences.

Dr. Bradbrook's and Dr. Hough's postscript strikes me as oddly inconsequent. Of course I believe that the intelligent need to meet and discuss; they need freedom to carry on a real intellectual intercourse, and it is desirable that they shouldn't have to feel, with apprehension, that a prepotent academicism means, authoritatively, something else by "real". As I have remarked, I have always found that those whom I myself should call the intelligent feel something very different from gratitude for "opportunities" of the kind they have been confronted with: they wondered how soon these "opportunities" will become flatly compulsory.

---

[1] In his first letter to the *TLS* (19-7-63) Mr. Noel, referring to the Ph.D. researcher, wrote ". . . the student is driven to the barren periphery of his subject in the desperate search to find something which has 'not been done' " and suggested that the doctoral dissertation should be turned "into a long essay on some topic of central importance to the student's field of study." In his second letter (2-8-63) Mr. Noel said: "The demand for higher education, and therefore for more university teachers, will inevitably grow, and if the universities are to avoid turning out 'substandard would-be researchers' they must abandon the notion that a Ph.D. thesis implies a publishable contribution to knowledge and substitute instead a profound competence in a particular field of study combined with a training in research gained through experience with a topic of importance and relevance, rather than of mere 'originality' ".

FROM QUALITY TO QUANTITY

As for Dr. Jack's proffered testimony that he knows me to be a bad influence[1] – his judging it a good thing to announce to the world that he has had as publishers' reader and as examiner, to give his voice against "followers" of me – I will only comment that his deciding to hazard that kind of allegation, which will be taken for a warning too, seems to me as injudicious a licence (if that's the word) as anyone wishing to establish his scholarly authority, and his weight as a witness in the present dispute, could well have indulged himself in.

I am, sir,
Very sincerely yours,
F. R. LEAVIS

---

[1] Dr. Jack criticised the scholarship of Dr. Leavis's research students. This letter was written in response to the letters which followed the publication in the *TLS* of Dr. Leavis's article "Research in English". The article can be found reprinted in *English Literature in our Time and the University* (Chatto and Windus, 1969).

43. *The Princess Casamassima*
To *The Spectator*: August 16, 1963

Sir, — Mr. Frank W. Bradbrook writes in your issue of August 9:

> "Whether one agrees with Dr. Leavis's views or not, it is necessary to recognise that they sometimes change. Thus, in his review of the latest volume of the *Oxford History of English Literature,* he refers to *The Princess Casamassima* as 'one of James's most embarrassing failures. . . so feeble a work that it wouldn't [couldn't — F.R.L.] have begotten anything.' In *The Great Tradition,* on the other hand, Dr. Leavis concludes his chapter on Henry James with a reference to the uncharacteristic 'earthy and sappy vitality' of *The Princess Casamassima,* deriving from Dickens."

One's views about some things in James's immense *oeuvre* will inevitably have changed if one has gone on reading him and thinking about him; but Mr. Bradbrook clearly means to assert that mine have changed about *The Princess Casamassima.* I can only reply that he is wrong and that he offers no evidence. The phrase he offers to quote from me is not evidence, for the use to which he puts it is either deliberately unscrupulous or culpably irresponsible, the intention in the conveying of which it figures in *my* context being the opposite of what he imputes. I have never had any but an adverse view of *The Princess Casamassima,* and when, away from home and books, I read Mr. Bradbrook's letter I wondered where on earth he had read that phrase in any context that he could have supposed to justify him. I couldn't remember having written on *The Princess Casamassima* at all. However, picking up a paperback copy of *The Great Tradition,* I find this single sentence about James's book:

> "And when, as in *The Princess Casamassima* (which brings so little comfort to those who would like to justify James by his interest in the class-war), he offers, uncharacteristically, something like an earthy and sappy vitality, it derives, significantly from Dickens."

I know, of course, of the wide agreement that I write badly, but I don't think I'm commonly charged with lack of care to be precise. If I had meant (with a marked inconsequence in the particular context, which deals with an apprehended basic 'deficiency' in James) to *credit* him with the uncharacteristic strength, I should have written: 'where he has achieved an earthy and sappy vitality. . . .' In what I did write (but Mr. Bradbrook did *not* quote when he *offered* to produce evidence against me) the verb is 'offers.' It is given a significant emphasis by the comma, and the parenthetic 'uncharacteristically,' and the phrase that follows is not Mr. Bradbrook's but mine: '*something like* an earthy and sappy vitality.' I am judging the appearance to be derivative from the Dickensian reality, and specious: surely that is plain enough.

It is true that I expect some closeness of attention from readers of my criticism, but I think that Mr. Bradbrook, his impulse and enterprise being what they were, was in honour obligated to give it.

He seems to think that there is relevant point in telling your readers that Professor Lionel Trilling has expressed a high opinion of *The Princess Casamassima*. Does Mr. Bradbrook mean that he shares it? Professor Trilling has also expressed a high opinion of the novels and the intellect of Sir Charles Snow. Does Mr. Bradbrook share that, too?[1]

Mr. R.G.G. Price himself concedes that Gosse's account of James's reaction to Beerbohm's parody is 'scarcely conclusive of the value of the parody.' More important − and more poignantly − it is scarcely conclusive as to the real effect on James. We know unequivocally, from that painfully moving letter how terribly poor James felt the accepted attitude to his work when it was expressed for the delectation of the reading public by the playful H. G. Wells.

For, in spite of what Mr. M. J. W. Higgins writes,[2] the attitude reinforced and stamped for ready currency by Beerbohm *was* the accepted attitude to James and his work. The 'convoluted style of James the Old Pretender's' novels was never in any case the fatuous elaboration of emptiness that Beerbohm's performance, 'The Mote in the Middle Distance,' makes it, and to suggest that it *was* such, an old and long-neglected great writer being in question, strikes me as neither funny nor decent. Neglected; the real genius ignored, as James had every reason, including the economic, for knowing. Think of that letter to the publishers − it should surely fill us with shame for our civilization when we read it − in which he concedes that there is nothing he can say against the melting-down of the plates of the collected edition of his works, the sales having been so utterly negligible. One would suppose from Mr. Higgins's letter that Beerbohm and Bloomsbury were merely discriminating against the unfortunate later development of an acclaimed and appreciated great master, on whose truly great things the author of *Zuleika Dobson*, or any member of Bloomsbury, was ready to write or

[1] The controversy over *The Princess Casamassima* broke out again. See letter 62.

[2] Mr. Higgins wrote that Beerbohm's "parody satirises the convoluted style of James the Old Pretender's 'late great novels' which 'Dr. Leavis dismisses.' "

talk intelligently. Let Mr. Higgins look up *Aspects of the Novel*: Mr. Forster there — and I know of no reviewer or literary intellectual who protested — talks of James in terms of *The Ambassadors*, as if *that* might fairly be taken as the representative work, although (I am not alone in thinking) it is the least rewarding of all the late novels. Another critical work of the period Mr. Higgins can easily lay hands on is *The Handling of Words*, by Vernon Lee, who also belonged to a milieu that combined social distinction with intellectual and literary culture. In that book she is explicitly guided by the consensus of the cultivated in her choice of the works she discusses, and she takes her sample of James from *The Ambassadors*.

I am, sir,

Very sincerely yours,

F. R. LEAVIS

44. Professor Trevor-Roper Criticises the University Examination System

To *The Sunday Times*: August 9, 1964

Sir, – Professor Trevor-Roper has done us a timely service in writing, and you in printing, the article "Questions of Degree" that appeared in *The Sunday Times* for August 2nd. More than one Director of Studies must have fought desperately, but in vain, to get the truths he calls our attention to understood, and effectively recognised, by a college governing body. A man who gets a first is a first-class man. And a first-class man – obviously, he's a man who gets a first. Professor Trevor-Roper bears his testimony against this delusive logic. What he reports, with a particular focus on history, I can corroborate from my own experience, which has been in English. And I have a graver sense of the concomitants and consequences than he, in his article, makes it his business to convey; from what he says, I can hardly doubt that he is aware of them. He puts well the indisputable basic facts:

(a) The qualities that enable a man to make a good show in an end-of-course examination against the clock are very different from those cultivated by a distinguished mind – one pre-eminently qualified by nature for higher education – that is intent on making the most of the opportunities one thinks of as offered by study at a university;

(b) The way to get a first is to study back-papers, invest in a cannily chosen minimum of "safe" topics, and get ready – practising, in doing so, a facility of adaptation such as may be required in the different foreseeable question-formulations – one's impressively allusive essays, each of a length that can be scribbled in three-quarters of an hour against the clock; and

(c) Though first-class men sometimes get firsts, it isn't their distinction that so avails – they are fortunate enough to have at command a journalistic facility that is not often found in men who know what real thinking (as opposed to the more or less sophisticated cliché-fluency that usually passes for thinking) is like.

I will say a little more under this last head, emphasising and developing a significance that remains implicit in Professor Trevor-Roper's article. History and English go together in this respect; pondering the nature of the thought proper to either study, and the criteria of quality of thought, one might say of either that it is at the other end of the scale from mathematics.

Thought in the literary field involves sensibility and value judgment.

Any real literary education entails the development of sensibility. One can't read with someone else's sensibility, and a judgment is one's own, or it is nothing. That is, there can be nothing schematic about the processes of thought belonging to literary study, and nothing demonstrable about their conclusions. Yet literary study, in so far as it deserves a place at the university, is essentially concerned with a discipline of thought.

To bring this truth home to a governing body composed predominantly of scientists is virtually impossible. They can't see why the class-list showing shouldn't, on the whole, be taken as an authoritative index of quality. If one at all often (and there is often reason) points out that A, who has a 11, is in fact alpha-plus — capable, that is, of distinguished original work — while B, who has a 1, has nothing but the kind of ability that succeeds in journalism or at the B.B.C., one's judgment soon ceases to carry much weight. One must expect to hear as a kind of refrain to one's life that tutorial authority has again thrown out the muttered menace, "the English men don't work hard enough" and one knows for certain that, in the official view, a good supervisor (or Director of Studies) is one who "gets firsts."

Better ways of determining a student's worth than the end-of-course race against the clock? — yes, such can be conceived, and such, indeed, have been proposed. But hardly discussed as matters of practical academic politics. Even in the days before the Robbins Report the actual reigning conditions were so forbiddingly adverse. And now, what hope can there be in the face of the catastrophic increase of numbers — an increase that must entail (I have met with no university teacher in my own subject or in history who questions it) a losing battle to maintain standards?

Intelligent methods of examination — the determination of a student's quality mainly by the quality of work done under conditions that allow him to show his power of thought and the real knowledge and promise developed in the years of study employed as they ought to be — implicitly postulate certain standards of personnel. I use the last word to cover not merely the teachers, but the students too.

A humane education that shall justify itself in terms of the idea of a university entails suitable students, enjoying (as no other kind can) the right kind of relations with suitable teachers. But long before the threat now represented by the Robbins Report became formidable it was plain that the old examination-system was automatically guaranteeing itself against any dangerous reform: to get a university post you must (among other things) have a first — and be acceptable to people whose position and distinction and self-esteem are a matter of their firsts being accepted at the official valuation.[1]

Yet at Cambridge, as at Oxford, there has still been the college. The more important kinds of "teaching" — of relations, that is, between seniors and undergraduates — have been a college responsibility. And this has made possible an effective resistance to *Gleichschaltung* — resistance to that reigning modern academicism which, as our civilization is going, becomes a more and more potent consensus of suggestion to the effect that intellectual distinction, in the humanities, manifests itself in journalistic brightness, glibness and unselfcritical confidence.

It has made possible the presence of centres of life in the university where intelligent young men can realise in decisively formative experience what a university is in so far as it is more than a collocation of specialist departments. For not merely is it an essential truth that, except as conscious and active members of an informal intellectual-social community, a man can't hope to arrive at any solution of the problem of making his studies a real education such as a university is supposed to offer; the more general truth is that only by providing — by being — a community of that kind can the university do anything towards a solution of the problem pointed to (without any perception of its nature) by Sir Charles Snow.

That is why I remained unco-operative in the face of insistent persuasion that I should take part in the "University of the Air." I won't lend myself in any way to the suggestion that university education is, or could be, a matter of being lectured to — of taking notes from an informative authority and following up his reading suggestions. "But why are the Colleges of Advanced Technology denied the name of universities?" asks the indignant Sir Charles Snow. It isn't enough to retort with "what's in a name?" When the name can be used in this way, the idea is well on the way to vanishing.

As for the college as maintaining in the university the effective presence of the Idea, everyone knows that the resisting power of the college is not what it was, and that the auguries don't favour any hope that it may increase. In my own subject we hear the enlightened

[1]Cf. "If you are a university teacher of English, naturally you are a certified distinguished intellectual, and you object very strongly to anything that throws doubt on that assumption," "The Outsider", *The Guardian,* June 13th, 1966.

advocacy of a reform by which the faculty – the university – should take over *all* teaching, and eliminate the licentious and injurious irregularity represented by the part (the major part) the college has up till now played.

Professor Trevor-Roper's observations, given the attention they deserve, bring us face to face with as momentous an issue as our civilization is confronted with – if, that is, one can properly talk of "confrontation" when the immense pressing fact we live with is a general non-recognition.

I am, sir,

Very sincerely yours,

F. R. LEAVIS

45. H. B. Parkes

To *The Times Literary Supplement*: September 17, 1964

Sir, – The closing paragraph of the front-page article in your issue for
September 10 begins: "Henry Bamford Parkes, as penetrating as usual in
analysis of his native culture. . .". Mr. Parkes, as a matter of fact, was
born and educated in England, having gone to an English Public School
and Oxford. It was because he was both inward with American life (he
became naturalized after having been for some years in the United
States) and able to observe it with an eye informed by English experience and education that the reports on America he wrote for *Scrutiny*
were found so different from American accounts of American literature
and civilization and so valuable.

I am, sir,
Very sincerely yours,
F. R. LEAVIS

46. Anti-industrial? Anti-political? Anti-scientific?
To *The Sunday Times*: November 1, 1964

Sir, — Mr Christopher Ricks, in reading and reporting on the book by
Dr Martin Green reviewed by him last Sunday, has clearly let an ill-
founded assumption convert itself into an allegeable fact: Dr Green can
hardly have intended to convey that he read English "under Dr Leavis."
I never, to my knowledge, met him while he was at Cambridge.

Mr Ricks ascribes to me an "anti-industrial, anti-political, anti-
scientific temper." "Anti-political"? — I signed the Liberal candidate's
nomination paper and subscribed to the Liberal election fund. "Anti-
industrial" and "anti-scientific"? — it seems to me that the implicit
argument here is that which led Sir Charles Snow to call Dickens, and
the writers who took Matthew Arnold's interest in civilization, Luddites.
I think it a pity that Mr Ricks should lend himself in any way to that
stupid and menacing ethos.

I am, sir,

Very sincerely yours,

F. R. LEAVIS

47. Association with Downing Annulled
To *The New Statesman*: July 30, 1965

Sir, — I see, to my surprise, in the *NEW STATESMAN* for 23 July that 'Leavis no longer teaches at Cambridge'. I have, in the past, learnt of facts that concern me nearly and very significantly from the press. But I have also read more authoritative statements than your contributor's that I have had the strongest grounds for believing unfounded — as, for instance, that which appeared as official in the *Telegraph* a week or two ago:

> 'Downing said in a statement regarding a re-election of a fellow: "The College is pleased that the original decision of last summer will now bear fruit, and there will not be, as we feared in the spring, a break in the teaching of English by a fellow of the College." '

The truth is the opposite of what might seem to be conveyed; the break now ensured will be of the completest kind. Your contributor's statement is, in its own way, equally unfounded.

He may have been told at Cambridge of arrangements made to ensure that I shall do no further teaching in the university either, but he would be unwise, I think, to credit such assurances; that they could be made effectively to 'bear fruit' seems to me inherently improbable. It is true that all association between me and Downing has been completely annulled. But, while I shall, during the next academic year, be spending half of each week at York, my intention is to go on being actively concerned in the teaching at Cambridge — actively enough to justify my continued membership of the Faculty Board.

I am, sir,

Very sincerely yours,

F. R. LEAVIS

48. The Misconceptions of Mr Bateson

To *The New Statesman*: January 7, 1966

Sir, – However sound F. W. Bateson's views about Oxford may be, on Cambridge he misinforms your readers. The 'Cambridge system', he says, 'is vitiated by its unhistorical bias.' The charge (that is its point) is an implicit assertion that the undergraduate reading English will, if he takes the prompting of the syllabus, have completed the Tripos believing that English Literature starts at the Renaissance. He will emerge innocent of any idea of 'English Literature from *The Owl and the Nightingale* to the present day' as a 'continuum', such innocence being fostered by an official innocence – the 'Cambridge fallacy': 'the failure to recognise' the truth that Mr. Bateson perceives and brings to our notice.

A glance at the syllabus for Part 1 would have sufficed – or, his pre-conceiving confidence disturbed (I hope) by my challenge, a second glance will now suffice – to disabuse Mr. Bateson of *his* innocence. Cambridge undergraduates he will see, have to take a paper that requires them to cultivate precisely the kind of knowledge of medieval literature that (in a way affecting me as not altogether unfamiliar) he indicates as real, possible and desirable. And he ought in candour, to admit that the scope of the paper has been determined in such a manner as to *insist* on the 'continuum'. Whatever the Middle English authorities feel about it (and Mr. Bateson mustn't expect them to show anywhere a unanimity of pleasure in so far as it promises to be effective), the encouragement to perceive the continuities that run back from Shakespeare into the centuries behind the Renaissance is – must be, when felt as real – an encouragement to read the creative literature of the Medieval period as creative literature; that is, to read it with appreciative intelligence. The Middle English authorities in general aren't (I believe) enthusiastic about John Speirs' work, but I have yet to hear of valid grounds for their warning their students against it. Let Mr. Bateson read *Chaucer the Maker, The Scots Literary Tradition*, and *Medieval English Poetry*, and, telling himself that this is essentially and significantly a product of Cambridge English, tell himself further that to grant this without seeing that the recognition disposes of the charge he has brought would be to show himself still unemancipated from Oxford.

If I have incurred the comment that it is a piece of presumption on my part, and in very bad taste, to speak, as I seem to do, for Cambridge, I can only point to the representative status assigned to me by Mr. Bateson in the close of his first paragraph: 'And literary instruction takes the place of religious instruction. They have their John Knox and we have our Dr. Leavis.'

Irony here? Well, perhaps — or even probably; but the first paragraph as a whole, reinforced by a great deal that follows, makes it plain that Mr. Bateson means his proposition, 'Literary instruction takes the place of religious instruction', with an unqualified seriousness. Let me then complete my vindication of Cambridge English and myself. The misrepresentation (though Mr. Bateson doesn't advance it as a charge) is certainly no more acceptable than that which I dealt with first, but, absurd as it is, it isn't as easily dealt with.

My best course, I think, is to focus on that word 'instruction'. No intelligent senior in an intelligently conceived English School, the word having been given the force implicit in Mr. Bateson's parallel of 'literary' and 'religious', would accept 'instruction' as describing his business. He is engaged, with his pupils and his colleagues, in the collaborative business that literary criticism, of its nature, is. He may 'tell' his pupils some facts; he will certainly tell them that a judgment (of value, significance, quality, thisness) is personal, or it is nothing, and that you can't take over a judgment or study literature without judging.

A real judgment, of course, means to be *more* than merely personal and the intention fulfils and justifies itself in the corrective and creative interplay that criticism entails. And I have never had cause to feel, or to suspect, that Catholics —or Methodists — couldn't, if qualified by interest and sensibility, be as collaborative in the critical-creative intercourse essential to university English as anyone else.

There, it seems to me, is where the emphasis should be laid by anyone concerned to win recognition for the urgent need of our civilization: the university as a humane centre or centre of consciousness and responsible human judgment, for the community. Mr. Bateson's account of literary education as a 'literary instruction' that replaces a 'religious' seems to me as infelicitous in its pregnancy of false suggestion as any coul be.

I am, sir,
Very sincerely yours,
F. R. LEAVIS

49. A Question of Standards

To *The Observer*: January 16, 1966

Sir, — My attention has been called to a review headed "All Terribly English" in which your reviewer writes: 'But in practice the way was soon open for Dr. Leavis to freeze his audience's young blood by telling them that a liking for P. G. Wodehouse indicates an incapacity to cope with "the important choices of life." '

Mr. John Gross's history is clumsy and unplausible fabrication, for all his inverted commas, and of a familiar kind. That Oxford conferred an honorary doctorate on P. G. Wodehouse is a fact — one on which, in *Scrutiny*, I made (another fact) my comment. When — it has been a rare passing allusion — I have mentioned Wodehouse since, my theme has been what it was in the first place: the *academic portent*.

There has never been question of an art or an influence to be taken in any way seriously; I should never have insulted an undergraduate audience (my habit being to address them as intelligent adults) by suggesting otherwise.

Mr. Gross, one deduces, feels that the portent should have been applauded, and regrets that Cambridge was forestalled. I, without disguise, think differently.[1]

I am, sir,

Very sincerely yours,

F. R. LEAVIS

[1] An interesting footnote to this letter is provided by R.C. Churchill's letter to the *TLS* for September 29 1972 in which he wrote: "I was the first journalist to defend P.G. Wodehouse against the false charge of treason during the war. But my article, "The Innocence of Dr. Wooster", was refused by half-a-dozen London journals in the spring of 1943 before eventually appearing, in an expanded version, in the Summer 1943 number of *Scrutiny*. . . . I doubt whether even Orwell, with his enviable command of the English language and his already great literary reputation could have got a defence of Mr Wodehouse into any London journal in 1943."

50. A Coterie Programme
To *The Oxford Review*: January 1966+

Sir, – Thank you for the copy of *The Oxford Review*. I gather that you
think I might at some time care to submit a contribution, and that you
would in any case like to have my comments. What I will do – while
my present misgivings hold it is all I can think of doing – is to ask some
questions. Why do you yourself, in the opening number, write, with
apparent assurance of a good reception, this: 'That A. C. Bradley has
worn better than Knights as a critic of Shakespeare is becoming a
commonplace.'?

Among whom is it becoming a commonplace, and how? – for, surely,
the arrival of such a proposition at the status of commonplace is in more
than one way odd. I don't think you are fair to L. C. Knights (if, for
instance, he had described *Macbeth* as a 'constatation of evil' instead of
a 'statement' – which without changing his intention he might have done
– your adverse commentary would have lost its plausibility.) It is not,
however, your treatment of Professor Knights I have primarily in view,
but the manifest will to revert to Bradley. I say 'will' because, though
you dismiss Knights's interest in Shakespeare as 'non-critical', nothing
you say in your article tends to make the aim of reinstating Bradley
critically respectable – to make it anything but pre- (or sub-) critical. Indeed, Bradley's own dealings with Shakespeare are themselves respectable compared with the kind of substitute for criticism that is implicit
in the attitude you identify yourself with.

If you want to know with full realization what kind of thing that
'criticism' is (for please believe that my 'implicit' is sincerely meant to
be courteous – an expression of candour in the old sense of the word),
I suggest that you study the major essay in the second number of the
Cambridge Quarterly, which came out at much the same time as your
own first number. It is entitled *'Scrutiny's* Failure with Shakespeare'
and it appears over the name of one of the Editors. To summarize his
argument would be difficult – and that *not*, for all local appearances to
the contrary, because it is closely or cogently argued. In fact, the essay
so little lends itself to discussion as criticism that it can hardly be discussed in any but a diagnostic spirit; that is, as an expression of the
parti pris that, mistaking itself for critical motivation, explains so odd,
laboured and confident a presentment of confusions, contradictions and
self-deceptions. The *parti pris* proclaims itself in the naively revealing
title: what, where the unprogrammed and unconcerted play of criticism

from a dozen writers over two decades upon the Shakespearean *oeuvre* is in question, would, or could, 'success' have been? This much at least the essay succeeds in making plain: the Shakespeare criticism published in *Scrutiny* doesn't, in the accuser's view, justify the conviction, shared (this being for him the '*Scrutiny* approach') by the very diverse critics, that the Bradley approach is inadequate and entails fallacious assumptions. It makes sufficiently plain, too, his view that the Editors (and more especially the present writer) deserve censure for having printed a great —or the greater — part of what actually appeared.

Positively, the following propositions can be safely attributed to the essayist:

(i) Bradley must be (has been?) vindicated against the criticism by which his authority and prestige have suffered, and he should now be brought back and reimposed.

(ii) There is also one other critic, a post-Bradleian, whose soundness and value deserve to be emphasized: Wilson Knight.

Now, sir, I am not suggesting that you yourself actually find it natural to associate advocacy of Bradley with advocacy of Wilson Knight. Nevertheless there is a significance for you (may I suggest?) in that Neo-Cambridge feat of patently unwitting self-exposure. Even so convinced, resolute and blind a servant of the *parti pris* as my accuser has (dimly enough) to admit that it won't do — that it wouldn't, in the face of so much distinctly post-Bradley work that can't be purged from our habit of thought, be tactful — to appear to be prescribing the Bradleian approach as by itself wholly adequate. If you ask why, with such perverse infelicity (for his own cause), he picks on Wilson Knight as the man to couple with Bradley, I am afraid that the answer must be a gesture towards the determined animus with which he labours to discredit Traversi — who was first published by *Scrutiny*. It found, in sum, a good many pages for him, and with critical reason. For, whatever criticism may be brought against Traversi's work, it is incomparably more disciplined than Wilson Knight's, and is always very much more worth discussion because of its concern for a kind of close relevance the very conception of which Bradley is precluded from by his approach — in spite of his ability (for Bradley was a cultivated reader of Shakespeare as well as a devoted one) to transcend on occasion the limitations imposed by his distinctive expository habit, focused as it was for character-analysis, and uncontrolled by anything like an adequate realization of the truth represented by the dictum (Eliot's): 'Poetic drama is something more than drama in verse'. Bradley tells us, 'The grave-diggers make us laugh', and he is in this significantly at one with Johnson, who says that 'the grave-diggers themselves may be heard with applause'.

As for Wilson Knight — but need I go on? We all recognize debts we owe for certain things in his early work, but can't fail to have registered the sad and embarrassing fact: the extravagantly privileged kind of creative interpretation he claimed the right to practise became very soon the complete and unresisting slave of an inspired private religion — too inspired to cultivate any useful relation with criticism or literature. The only trait that relates Wilson Knight with Bradley is a sentimental idealising romanticism.

By way of enforcing the point of these references to the *Cambridge Quarterly* I will now quote a brief passage from your essay:

'What modern Shakespeare scholar has given evidence of having responded as profoundly or humanly to Shakespeare as Pope or Johnson? Do we have Shakespeare as a genuine possession, and in what ways does our greater information help us to possess Shakespeare as fully as Johnson did?'

You will, I hope, forgive my saying that the critical implications of this line of talk are so absurd that, knowing the elaboration of much the same line to be a habit of the anti-*Scrutiny* essayist and his associates, I can't but see significance in the identity. I greatly admire Johnson, and should like to think that I have proved it. But it is certainly absurd to make him the ideal critic of Shakespeare, or to speak of him as one who possessed Shakespeare fully. Though he may sometimes seem to transcend them in non-evaluative characterization of Shakespeare's use of the English language, critically he doesn't escape the limitations of his age: creative expression — the Shakespearean poetic creativity that so utterly and unmistakably defies paraphrase — defeats (or is defeated by) the critical apparatus of preconceptions, assumptions and habits that Johnson brings up. A major consequence is that he can, quite unequivocally (*pace* the Cambridge essayist, who resorts to dishonest and falsifying selectiveness in 'proving' the contrary) exalt Shakespeare's comedy above his tragedy. No critic who does that can be said to possess Shakespeare fully.

The relation between this plain major 'failure with Shakespeare' on Johnson's part and the confident eighteenth-century naïveté about the possibilities of expression in language is made perfectly clear in the half-dozen paragraphs of the Preface beginning: 'In tragedy his performance seems constantly to be worse, as his labour is more'. Note the 'constantly': Johnson is not pointing to occasional bad patches. And note

121

the Johnsonian felicity of this:

'It is incident to him to be now and then entangled with an un-
wieldy sentiment, which he cannot well express, and will not reject; he struggles with it awhile, and if it continues stubborn,
comprises it in words such as occur, and leaves it to be disentangled
and evolved by those who have more leisure to bestow upon it'.

Johnson is unable to think that any valid piece of poetic expression
could be describable as 'comprising' subtle and complex 'sentiment' in
'words such as occur'. A responsible poet gets his ideas clear, and then
uses his Judgment in finding words to express them — lucidly, gram-
matically and with decorum. Thus for Johnson Shakespeare moves
between 'natural' comic dialogue (at which his genius excels) and de-
clamatory eloquence, and we readily understand the superlative reference
to *The Mourning Bride*.

In any case, how much allegeable Shakespeare criticism did Johnson
write? What is there is the Preface that one would resort to as worth
pondering in relation to any serious challenge one had taken up from a
given work or aspect of Shakespeare? What in the notes to the plays is
there (apart from fallacious promptings) that repays critical attention?
The lauded characterization of Falstaff deals with him as if he were an
actual person, and ignores his specific and essential value in the total
creative work. One thinks of Bradley discussing Iago, and deciding that,
though not so great in wickedness as Napoleon, he is greater than Milton's
Satan. It is easy to understand why the Neo-Cambridge Neo-Classicizing
crusade associates Johnson and Bradley in its orthodoxy.

If anything further needs saying to enforce the point of my making
these references to the *Cambridge Quarterly*, let me remind you that
one of the members of your advisory Board (the literary member) is also
an Editor of that journal. Another Editor is reported as having opened
a course of lectures with a theme that can be summarized as 'Since
Bradley, Shakespeare criticism has steadily declined'.

Beware then of coterie-commonplaces — for where such absurdities
impose themselves as currency (that is, are 'becoming commonplaces')
you may suspect conditions of genesis such as are focused in coteries.
And it is astonishing how imperceptibly the process of 'becoming' can
spread and take hold, and what mischief it can do. I see that I have
moved, after all, towards offering advice, but I will stop at the note of
warning. A literary Editor, then, needs to be peculiarly on his guard
against any suggestion of a coterie-programme; a critical policy is not
that kind of thing at all. It demands a fiercely suspicious alertness in the

face of a world (literary-academic) where things are more or less subtly 'becoming commonplaces'. And such an alertness implies both a conscious and real grasp of critical fundamentals and (what that, in fact, entails) a genuine concern to cultivate in oneself a finely responsive sensibility.

Of course, you agree with me here. But note that the Cambridge exposer of *Scrutiny* is capable of seeing a superiority of Wilson Knight to Traversi in the former's *'passionately disinterested and direct absorption in Shakespeare's art'*, and then of adding (aimed at Traversi) this: 'But no mere external habit of "approach" will help a writer who hasn't the root of the matter in him'. The 'root of the matter' with which Wilson Knight is credited, the 'passionately disinterested and direct absorption in Shakespeare's art', obviously entails what I have called a finely responsive sensibility, and, equally obviously, a disciplined and delicate concern for relevance. Actually, Wilson Knight's 'absorption' is a matter — he himself is explicit about it — of his claiming the right to rely on his discipline-free intuition and his 'passionate' creative afflatus, so much so that he ignores all questions of authenticity: if a text appears in the collected 'Shakespeare', then it *is* Shakespeare — for Wilson Knight's purposes. As for the nature of those purposes, they, like his method, are indeed very different from Traversi's. 'It is significant' I remarked (I see) in reviewing one of Wilson Knight's earlier books for *Scrutiny*, 'that he should not question his ability to approach Dante and Goethe on the same easy terms as Shakespeare. Something of them, of course, will get through in translation, but Professor Knight shows not the least sign of uneasiness at having to rely on Cary's *Divine Comedy* and Professor Latham's *Faust*. In the poetry of his own language his procedure is truly shocking; and any text will do so long as it yields a congenial or convenient "content"... he will cap Dante and Shakespeare with the Browning of *Abt Vogler* and the Tennyson of *In Memoriam* — worse, he actually quotes for the sake of "content" some stanzas from the disastrously bad part of *The Palace of Art*. He seems, in fact, completely indifferent about quality — realized value: the general paraphrasable meaning, if it fits the argument, is good enough. On page 40 we read, incredulously, "...Kent in *Lear*, Horatio in *Hamlet*, Osborne in *Journey's End*." ' I might have added that his ability to adduce Flecker's *Hassan* in the same spirit and the same impartial way is wholly characteristic.

And yet the *parti pris* is potent enough to stupefy your Cambridge *confrère* into making Wilson Knight (who once, in his best days, told me that his business was interpretation *as opposed to* criticism) a paragon of docile sensibility, disinterested submission to his text and superlatively close relevance — *the* criterion, in fact, where corrective rigour is to be applied to the unacceptable post-Bradley Shakespearian. You are confident that you couldn't yourself be betrayed into absurdities as gross and unashamed? How then can you explain your ability to make Johnson the exemplar of a 'full possession' of Shakespeare? A great deal more than Shakespeare criticism is involved in that judgment, as the Cambridge essayist and his associates have demonstrated. If you really mean it, and stand by it, then there is little reason for supposing you incapable of offering to establish an inferiority in Henry James by reading out, for comparison (I have heard it done), a passage of David Storey, or of thinking it sufficient, when bent on dismissing Hopkins, to send your pupils for the critical grounds to Yvor Winters, who sees the poetic real thing in Robert Bridges and his daughter.

And can you be unaware that in America, where it was solemnly inaugurated, the crusade for Neo-Classicism has petered out in bankruptcy?

I do indeed think there is an urgent need to have an intelligent and disinterested critical organ. Please believe that, and take this answer to your invitation for a proof. The more deeply one feels the need, the more wary is one of being made to appear benign, or neutral, in the face of what aims, essentially — not the less so for deferential shows, at the undoing of all one has worked for. And it seems proper to add that I, having been habitually pretty free with my trust, have had in my 'retired' years some seismic shocks of disillusion.

I am, sir,

Very sincerely yours,

F. R. LEAVIS

+ Dr. Leavis has supplied the following note to this letter: "This was written in response to an editorial request, accompanied by a copy of the first number of the short-lived *Oxford Review*, for a contribution. The fact that the officially avowed Literary Adviser to the new review was also one of the editors of *The Cambridge Quarterly* (itself very young) occasioned a long delay between the Oxford editor's receiving the article and his finally intimating that he would like to print it — a little modified. The total passage of time was such that there seemed no point by then in sending for future publication a reply to what had appeared in the first number of *The Cambridge Quarterly* — to which there had been strong reasons for not sending it in the first place. *The Oxford Review* soon ceased to appear".

51. *The Cambridge Quarterly*
To *The Times Literary Supplement*: February 17, 1966

Sir, – Under the title "Dutiful Heirs" you printed two or three weeks ago an article conveying an explicit and very confident suggestion which is utterly unfounded. I had nothing to do with the conception, encouragement or planning of the *Cambridge Quarterly*, and if I appear in the first number it certainly does not follow that I wrote an essay for the new review, or did anything but yield to urgent requests for permission to print a lecture.

I asked the editors to disabuse your public of the misconception fostered by your article and the appearance of my lecture in the opening place as the major contribution in the new review, but it has been brought home to me that the letter you printed from Mr. Shapira leaves it generally assumed that I am in the editorial confidence and may be counted on to be a regular, or frequent, contributor. On the contrary: the editorial body itself most certainly does not suppose me to be in resonance with it in regard to ethos or policy, and my essay is not a first contribution by a member of the connexion. I can make that quite plain by saying that it will be found to be my last.

I am, sir,

Very sincerely yours,

F. R. LEAVIS

52. The Bibliographical Check-List of Dr. Leavis's Writings
To *The Times Literary Supplement*: August 25, 1966

Sir, — Referring to that constituent of the "check-list" of my writings which he exempts from his severest comments, your reviewer (August 18) says that "possibly" it was compiled "with the cooperation of Dr. Leavis himself". In fairness to the compilers I am bound to state that they had no help from me and, in fairness to myself as well and to the causes I should wish my name to be associated with, that I had no part at all in the scheme, of which, as represented by the publication you review, I was ignorant. I knew of a normal kind of academic undertaking, involving no one but the two students from abroad, who were doing for academic reasons what was no concern of mine. That my publishers should publish it I never conceived possible, since the only kind of printing-press in view as an eventual possibility was a departmental one at the disposal of one of the compilers. The "good-hearted" disposal of royalties[1] referred to by your reviewer did not, and could not, come up because neither royalties nor a publishing house had any relevance to what was intended — I am pretty sure that no such idea had entered the minds of the compilers at the time, nor should I ever have countenanced such a thing.

I am, sir,
Very sincerely yours,
F. R. LEAVIS

[1] "All royalties and profits will be given to the fund opened by the F.R. Leavis Lectureship Trust to found in Cambridge a Lectureship in English Literature bearing the name of Dr. Leavis." — from the preface to the *Check-List*.

53. To Reform the Annanite Reformer

To *The Times*: January 22, 1968

Sir, — Lord Annan, in his letter (January 19), exhibits, as stern admonisher, the strength and the courage of representativeness: the world, he knows, is with him. The menace with which he backs his injunction to the universities is not an idle one. In fact, there is no more urgent duty soliciting those who are concerned for the real interests of the community than to resist the blind forces Lord Annan so confidently points to.

Of course, we all know that desperate crises may call for desperate measures — for recourses that wouldn't seem capable of defence unless we told ourselves they were very strictly ad hoc and exceptional. But Lord Annan, while invoking the immediate crisis, makes it plain that the step he prescribes is to be a commitment to a permanent surrender — surrender of something he identifies with 'privilege'.

The universities, he says, 'could offer to lay on residential courses of a month's length in the summer for children who would have stayed on at school but for the postponement. . . .' Reassuring us with the datum that the 'drop-out rate among such teen-age students is very high', he tells us: 'A month's intensive teaching might work wonders and enable more to qualify' — i.e., to pass examinations. But why, one asks, should university teachers be supposed to be qualified for that kind of cramming, which is utterly at odds with the qualifications that, as university teachers, they have in long experience acquired, and by reading, thought, pondered experience and hard work continually renew and bring up to date?

Lord Annan, with the menace-enforced 'must' of the following, provides the answer: 'If the universities are not to be attacked as citadels of privilege, they must give what help they can.' We are to understand that, in the near future, there will be the closest relation between a university teacher's qualifications and those needed for the emergency; helping let-down teen-agers to 'qualify' in spite of their having not been prevented from leaving school at 15 — coaching them for their examinations — will be immediately relevant training: 'When the sixth-form curriculum is reformed, they (the universities) will have to provide more elementary teaching for their own students, and it would be useful to get experience in providing it.'

The 'privilege' the universities must surrender lest they be attacked as anti-democratic citadels is the right (or duty) to maintain the

127

standards proper to a university. Of course 'university' now, in this country, too, is a term applied to some very different kinds of thing – there is, for instance, the Open University, there are correspondence colleges that hope to become universities, and Mr Wilson not long ago expressed his satisfaction that a number of Colleges of Technology had swelled the total of universities (a snub for snobbery, he thought).

Lord Annan's letter (he is still a Provost) exemplifies the dangers associated with this liberal use of the term. Essential truths have been almost forgotten. Firstly, the phrase 'the standards proper for a university' means something. Secondly, to identify the problem of Higher Education with the idea of the university is disastrous; for, thirdly, if standards are not maintained at the university the advance of Higher Education will (for one thing) be grievously disabled.

Neither democratic zeal nor egalitarian jealousies should be permitted to dismiss or discredit the fact that only a limited proportion of any young adult age group is capable of profiting by, or enjoying, university education. The proper standards can be maintained only if the students the university is required to deal with are – for the most part, at any rate – of university quality. If standards are not maintained somewhere the whole community is let down.

I am, sir,
Very sincerely yours,
F. R. LEAVIS

54. "The Bloke George Eliot Lived With"
To *The Times*: April 2, 1968

Sir, – The concluding sentence of the front-page essay in your *Saturday Review* for March 30 runs: "Or was their exceptional union, what Dr. F. R. Leavis has exasperatedly called a 'high-falutin' *tête-à-tête*,' and they embarrassedly called a 'communion of the soul,' a total marriage, so that George Eliot was joint flesh, joint mind and experience, of George Lewes and Marian Evans?" I read this with even more astonishment than I had read the title of the essay ("The bloke George Eliot lived with"), for not only was what was imputed to me something worse than crass vulgarity, but I knew that I had never referred to George Eliot's relations with Lewes in any way that could have remotely suggested it. An equally astonished reader of the article was finally, after a search, able to bring to my attention this in *The Great Tradition* (pages 75-6):-

"But the show of presenting this haze from the outside soon lapses; George Eliot herself, so far as Dorothea is concerned, is clearly in it too. That is peculiarly apparent in the presentment of those impossibly high-falutin' *tête-à-tête* – or soul to soul – exchanges between Dorothea and Will, which is utterly without irony or criticism."

I give as illustration of the "tone and quality" of the exchanges one of Ladislaw's utterances. For making such a passage of literary criticism a ground for representing me as calling George Eliot's life with G. H. Lewes a "high-falutin' *tête-à-tête*" I see no excuse.

I am, sir,

Very sincerely yours,

F. R. LEAVIS

55. The Function of the University at the Present Time
To *The Times*: October 8, 1968

Sir, — In your leading article "The British Backlash" (October 5) there is one thing that is not said, and that the most important. In its absence what you do say gives ground only for despair. "Student revolt" can't be intelligently discussed as an isolated thing. Popular resentment generated by student violence and fatuity may lead to greater firmness in the universities (and I hope there will be firmness), but that won't itself cure the disease there; and elsewhere all the familiar manifestations — violence, wanton destructiveness, the drug menace, adolescent promiscuity, permissiveness, the enlightened praise of the young for their "candour" about sex — will go on unabated. To isolate "student revolt" is to promote blankness about the nature of the disease — and blankness is a major manifestation.

There is no simple remedy and no possibility of a rapid cure. But your leading article might properly have pointed out that in default of a more positive and intelligent conception of the university and its role in civilization than is entertained by (say) Lord Robbins and Lord Annan, or any influential politician who has made his views known, not only is there no hope of ending "student unrest", there is no hope that the first of the three problems listed by Mr. Cecil King several columns across the page from your leading article will begin to be tackled. It is (he says) the problem "how to establish a moral authority at the centre which will give our young people leadership, and contain the rising tide of crime".

That is not an adequate conception of the problem, which is one of cultural disinheritance and the meaninglessness of the technologico-Benthamite world: to state it as Mr. Cecil King does amounts to saying that nothing can be done about it. And in fact nothing will be done unless society commits itself to a sustained creative effort of a new kind — the effort to re-establish an educated, well-informed, responsible and influential public — a public that statesmen, administrators, editors, and newspaper proprietors can respect and rely on as well as fear. Society's only conceivable organ for such an effort is the university, conceived as a creative centre of civilization.

I am, sir,
Very sincerely yours,
F. R. LEAVIS

56. The Criticism of Chaucer's Poetry
To *The New Statesman*: December 13, 1968

Sir, – Dr Derek Brewer, by way of enforcing his observation that in the 20th century 'British scholarship and criticism has had relatively little taste for Chaucer', writes: 'Nor has Dr Leavis yet fulfilled the intention, expressed a long time ago, of commenting on Chaucer.' Will he tell us where he finds that intention expressed? If he thinks that by turning up the *Scrutiny* article, 'Sociology and Literature' (reprinted in *The Common Pursuit*) he will be able to put his finger on some justifying passage or phrase, he ought (I must warn him) to be prepared for disappointment. I have never entertained any such intention. That is not to say that I haven't thought Chaucer a very great poet who ought to be much more current than he is, and haven't expressed these views in speech habitually. But, as Dr Brewer might have gathered from the article to which I have referred, I think that to write on Chaucer one needs to have not only an intelligent and cultivated interest in English poetry, but some specialist equipment too. My taste, and that of the inner *Scrutiny* circle generally, for Chaucer was expressed in our welcoming the opportunity to print the admirably qualified John Speirs: the substance of his book *Chaucer the Maker* was written for *Scrutiny* and appeared there first.

I am, sir,
Very sincerely yours,
F. R. LEAVIS

57. English Studies and Student Unrest[1]
To *The Times Literary Supplement*: June 12, 1969

Sir, — I am not capable of supposing that anyone who expresses his extreme horror at the facts of Auschwitz, Dachau and Belsen is anything but sincere and very earnestly moved. When, therefore, the evocation of those facts passes so easily into that way of referring to my insistent and argued contention which I have commented on — the contention that a new kind of creative effort on the part of society is called for of which the university is the only conceivable organ, the easy passage strikes me as a disagreeable lapse — a lapse into irresponsibility. If Professor Daiches (or Dr. Steiner) thinks that in using "mime" to express my sense of the irresponsibility I use too offensive a word, I undertake, should the address ever be reprinted, to find another. But that must still express my adverse and strongly felt judgment.

The general blankness about the nature of the menace in view, the impossibility of reducing any adequate statement to such terms as might, perhaps, lend themselves to helpful journalistic use or of supposing that anyone could responsibly prescribe a simple remedy, and the frightening difficulty of getting any recognition at all for what one was actually proposing, were insistent themes of my address. To pass from Belsen to remarking, with an intimation of pondered, informed and wondering dissent, that I ("as every one knows" implied) make large claims for the study of literature is not to advance serious consideration of the urgent problem that faces us here and now, in our own country, or of the case I have in fact presented: the effect is the reverse.

I have been assuming that my memory is not at fault when it tells me that I read a review of Dr. Steiner's book by Professor Daiches in which he picked on the reference to my own alleged attitude, and identified himself with the attitude formulated, with its implication, by the author. And there you have my point; I was illustrating the way in which dissuasive and indolent misconception is perpetuated; an intellectual in high repute is corroborated by an equally well-known

---

[1] Dr. Leavis is replying here to the large correspondence which resulted from the publication of his lecture " 'English' — Unrest and Continuity" in the *TLS* (it was reprinted in *Nor Shall My Sword,* Chatto and Windus, 1972). In the lecture Dr. Leavis criticised "the profundity of solemn doubt mimed by Dr. Steiner and Professor Daiches" who had contended that since Literary Studies had not prevented the German Concentration Camps, they could not perform the function Dr. Leavis wished of them.

academic humanist.

So to Mr. Malcolm Pittock I must reply that I do *not* in my address contend that the "study of literature is necessarily a comprehensively civilizing process", or anything that can reasonably be summarized in that way. Of course, in referring briefly to complexities one has to simplify, but Mr. Pittock's simplification eliminates my essential theme and ignores my argument. As for student unrest, I do indeed know that even in this country − and it was to the situation in this country that I explicitly addressed myself − there are some respectable motives and impulsions behind some of it. But I have also to state that my experience or judgment or both must be taken to differ radically from Mr. Pittock's.

I had hoped I had made it plain that I didn't regard America's "strength", with its conditions and concomitants, as a matter for simple attitudes of approval or disapproval, pleasure or displeasure. Such simple attitudes − and that was an insistence of mine − are out of place in the world of complexities and ambiguities in which we have to determine what stance our sense of personal responsibility dictates.

I hope I may contradict Margaret Drabble and say that I am not sorry, but glad, to learn that she did, after all, work for her Tripos. I think that she may have been a victim of the kind of simplification incident to journalism, and that the statement I remember to have read may have come from a chatty summary of a summary. But − and this was the point I wanted to enforce − that some people get Firsts in English without having done any serious work is widely believed among undergraduates at Cambridge, and undergraduates carry the belief out into the world with them.

I have read Miss Patricia M. Watson's letter with interest.[1]

I am, sir,
Very sincerely yours,
F. R. LEAVIS

---

[1] Miss Watson, a student at the University of Stirling, wrote to praise the English course there.

58. The Filming of *Women in Love*
Quoted from a private letter in *The Times*: November 8, 1969

Sir, — I cannot countenance in any way that Lawrence's *Women in Love* (or Eliot's *Four Quartets*) *could* be filmed, or that there could be any profit in arguing with 'transposers' (translaters, adapters?) who assumed otherwise. Lawrence himself *wrote Women in Love*. It's an obscene undertaking to 'write it again' for the screen. . . . No one who had any inkling of the kind of *thing* the novel is, or how the 'significance' of a great work of literature is conveyed, or what kind of thing the significance is, could lend himself to such an outrage. Great writers, even when they're dead, ought to be protected.

I am, sir,

Very sincerely yours,

F. R. LEAVIS

59. The Blankness of the Intellectual Community
To *The Times*: April 28, 1970

Sir, — I hope I can echo the opening sentence of your today's leader about my Bristol lecture without seeming to indulge in ungracious irony —it is the leader itself that is the "heartening sign".[1] The heartening significance gets an emphasis from the contrast with the routine reference your Economics Editor, Mr. Peter Jay, made to the lecture in your last issue. I say "routine" because he hadn't felt called on to pay any attention to the argument of the lecture: he knew beforehand with what kind of gesture it was safe to dismiss it, and he felt he knew, as an economist and a trained mind, what "human responsibility" was — and that I could be relied on to question his competence.

It is not mere vanity that leads me to assure you that my lecture doesn't express anything like a new awareness on my part of "what is at stake". *Education and the University* came out more than a quarter of a century ago, and it summed up the preoccupations of years — known and explicit preoccupations justifying (he feels) the Cambridge ex-Professor[2] when, in his memoirs, he makes his historical reference to the notorious nuisance the "Leavisites" were in his time. And in a number of published lectures of the past three or four years[3] I have emphasized the blankness of the "intellectual community" in face of the menace as the most frightening characteristic of our plight.

I have reason, then, for welcoming your leader, and attributing great importance to it.

I am, sir,

Very sincerely yours,

F. R. LEAVIS

---

[1] The excellent leader "Counter-attack" began: "Dr. Leavis's lecture at Bristol on " 'Literarism' versus 'Scientism' ", printed in *The Times Literary Supplement* this week, is a heartening sign." (*The Times* 24–4–70)

[2] Basil Willey

[3] The lectures have been collected in *Nor Shall My Sword* (Chatto and Windus, 1972)

60. The Compassion of Lord Annan

To *The Times Literary Supplement*: May 7, 1970

Sir, – One thing, at any rate, emerges from Lord Annan's reply (April 30) to my lecture[1] : he desires – intensely desires – to have it understood that the letter he wrote to *The Times* proposing that the universities should "lay on" vacation courses for the cramming of what are now called teenagers did *not* deserve the commentary I made on it in my answering letter to *The Times*[2] . He believes (unlike me), he says, in "pluralism and compassion": that proposal, we are to understand, was a fling of compassion – something not to be taken as a characteristic expression of his habitual attitude towards, and conception of, the university.

The other thing that might be said to emerge clearly is the insistent explicitness with which he declares his devotion to the intellect. "Universities" – this is the clinching proposition he offers us – "should hold up for admiration the intellectual life." I myself think this, offered as the essential emphasis, hardly a felicity. But the point to be made regards the self-contradiction in which Lord Annan is inescapably involved – a self-contradiction that would itself have been enough to explain why it should be so impossible to find any coherent argument in his set-piece.

He brings in the theme of reforms decreed for enforcement in the sixth-form curriculum, implying that they have been at issue between us, and that they may now be relevantly made a matter for a significant challenge to me – a challenge to say clearly at last where I stand in regard to them. But actually the only way in which they had come up had been that, in his now notorious letter to *The Times*, he adduced them as among the menacing prospects that should make the dons in their citadels of privilege think twice before doing anything but yield to the pressures of advancing democracy: cramming those unenthusiastic children for their "qualifying" exams would, he said, be good practice for the unaccustomed kind of work they would *have* to do when the reformed sixth form curriculum came into force. My only comment regarded not the postulated imminent reforms but Lord Annan's

[1] The lecture, entitled " 'Literarism' versus 'Scientism': The Misconception and the Menace" is reprinted in Dr. Leavis's book *Nor Shall My Sword,* (Chatto and Windus, 1972).

[2] See Letter 53.

attitude and its significance, which was to the effect that dons must learn to forget their privileged fussiness about the intellectual standards proper to a university: they must serve society.

He is profoundly aware of criticism to which he is exposed. His uneasiness comes out in his tactics. Thus he hopes to pose me with the question whether I think it a pity York University was founded. The truly relevant reply is that in English, in which York is in a position to be very selective – and in regard to which I can testify, out of some intimate acquaintance, the standard of students is high – work at university level is possible, to the pleasure and profit of students and teachers and the advantage of the university. This is all I will, or need, say about York in reply to Lord Annan's tactical use of my known connection. But I will add that I have talked with many university teachers from many universities and I have seldom talked with one who did not comment on the problems and disabilities caused by the depressingly large presence at the university of students who were not university material.

For the advocates of the comprehensive university, of course, the last phrase is meaningless. Lord Annan, to judge by his article, would prefer to be thought of as taking a decidedly different line. I shall be favourably impressed by that suggestion when Lord Annan publicly and decisively repudiates the conception of enlightenment, democracy and progress voiced by Mr. Fowler[1], Minister of State, and Mr. Christopher Price, M.P. The last-named says in his letter to the *TLS* (April 30) that he "simply knows that the demand for all forms of higher education. . .is growing apace", and he merely "wants to plan for this inevitable demand". I still think that he is, as I said, "innocent", in that he, at any rate, is not consciously disingenuous. The direction in which his idea of the "inevitable demand" drives may be seen in his article on enlightened Sweden ("Sweden's New Comprehensiveness") in last week's *New Statesman*. The late Kingsley Martin, it will be recalled, writing towards the end of his life, on Sweden as the ideal civilized society, observed in a puzzled way that the Swedes, very curiously, didn't seem to be happy.

Lord Annan himself thinks it safe to dismiss my use of the word "creative" with easy mockery, and to be, in a light intellectual way,

---

[1] Mr. Fowler in a public speech complained that Dr. Leavis seemed to believe in a "finite pool of talent." Mr. Fowler presumably believes in an *infinite* pool of talent, even of university material. See *The Times*, May 16, 1970 p.2.

merely amused by the phrase "collaborative creative effort". And the letters you, sir, have selected to print will assure him that he has the kind of support he needs. "There never was a golden age of an 'organic' community" — the misrepresentation that dismisses my concern and my argument in that way is not his invention: it is a routine among the enlightened. As Lord Annan invokes it, it is his dismissive reply (he offers nothing more like a reply) to my observation that "organic" is a necessary word, for which the technological age proposes to have no use.

There is, then, little reason why he should find himself disputing the claim that a computer can write a poem. It is, in culturally influential circles, coming to be accepted as a valid one. Thus in Friday's *Times* Mr. Peter Jay, Economics Editor, expressing poised surprise at my challenge, informs his public that, having re-read and reconsidered my lecture, he still "sees no insuperable conceptual difficulty about a computer writing a poem". Lord Annan himself, I am pretty sure, in the cultural milieu from which he takes his colour, could safely commit himself to the same position. In fact, I suspect that letters will have been received[1] in the *TLS* office to the effect that the questioning of the claim is ignorant, prejudiced, out-of-date and indefensible.

I am, sir,

Very sincerely yours,

F. R. LEAVIS

[1] They had.

61. T. S. Eliot's Final Judgment of Pound's *Cantos* (2)
To *The Times Literary Supplement*: September 11, 1970

Sir, — I should like to make a correction to the letter of mine you print in the current *TLS* (August 28).[1] Being in a hurry to catch the post, and not being able to find Eliot's letter, which was missing from where I had supposed it to be, I trusted to my memory in reporting what he had written about the *Cantos*. Later, having found that "boring" occurs twice on page 190 of the Penguin *New Bearings*, I began to wonder, though I was quite certain about the emphatic corroboration, whether he had actually conveyed it by just taking up that word from me. My misgiving is confirmed now that I have Eliot's letter in front of me. After referring to another matter, Eliot continues:

> This gives me the opportunity for saying that I have read with interest the epilogue to the paperback edition of *New Bearings*. I agree with you about Pound & the aridity of the *Cantos*, with the exception of at least one item & a few lines from one of the so-called Pisan *Cantos* where it seems to me also that a touch of humanity breaks through; I mean the lovely verse of "Bow (sic) down thy vanity" and the reference to the Negro who knocked him up a table when he was in the cage at Pisa. And of course Pound's incomparable sense of rhythm carries a lot over. But I do find the *Cantos*, apart from that exceptional moment, quite arid and depressing.

With this sentence Eliot's letter ends.

I am, sir,
Very sincerely yours,
F. R. LEAVIS

---

[1] In this letter, which is not reprinted here, Dr. Leavis said that T.S. Eliot had judged the *Cantos* to be "boring".

62. Henry James and Dickens

To *The Times Literary Supplement*: March 5, 1971

Sir, – Mr. Gorley Putt, in his letter (February 19) starts by adducing in a way that reverses my clear intention a critical observation I made about *The Princess Casamassima* thirty-four years ago. Referring to what I say about James's novel in the chapter on *Little Dorrit* in *Dickens the Novelist*, he writes:

> This view, consonant with his dismissal of the novel as "feeble" and "one of James's most embarrassing failures". . ., but quite discordant with his still earlier view (*Scrutiny*, Vol. V, No. 4, 1937) that the novel *has* "an earthy and sappy vitality", is now put forward with a vehemence that has little to do with *Little Dorrit* and nothing to do with certain known facts in James's writing life.

I find that what I actually wrote in 1937 (*Scrutiny*, Vol. V, p. 416) was:

> . . .something of the effect of *The Portrait of a Lady* is suggested there. And when, as in *The Princess Casamassima* (which brings so little comfort to those who would like to justify James by his interest in the class-war) he *offers*, uncharacteristically, *something like* an earthy and sappy vitality, it derives, significantly (it might be said), from Dickens, a literary source.

It will be observed that what I wrote was, not "has", but "offers", and that, followed as it is by the "something like" which Mr. Putt leaves out, and to which the context gives the clear force of "an unconvincing show of", conveys a severely adverse judgment, besides stating my case that he is there parasitic on Dickens. Where is the "discordance"?

And I can't see why Mr. Putt should suppose that his biographical remarks and his autobiographical quotations have anything to do with criticism. We all know that James walked about London, and are willing to believe that he was disagreeably impressed by the squalor and misery that met his eyes. But it is literary criticism that is in question, and a critic arrives at his judgments by bringing to bear his intelligence and sensitiveness on his author's text. How can anyone fail to perceive that at any social level much lower than the highest James was disablingly a foreigner? He may have walked about with (as Mr. Putt says) "his eyes open" – no doubt he heard much low talk; but his offer to render "low" speech is as embarrassing as the late T. S. Eliot's. That alone is enough to make his low life "impossible", and it goes with the revealing innocence with which he alleges that a Hyacinth Robinson, escaped for the first time from the Cockney world in which he had been brought up, could, in spite of his inevitable speech, undernourished physique, dress and everything else Cockney about him, pass at that date among "county" visitors at the Princess's country mansion as a gentleman.

It is natural that the Dickensian genius, which renders so irresistibly an un-Jamesian at-home-ness in the total English world, should have prompted James to make his offer at a similar enterprise, and not at all paradoxical, since he was venturing into fields where he was hopelessly an outsider, that when he thought he had an original theme he could only incarnate it by appropriating Dickens. That *The Princess Casamassima* has this kind of radical dependence on *Little Dorrit* is made plain by the elaborate but feeble complex of borrowings and echoings that we have to recognize when we compare the two novels. There is the prison and the young protagonist whose early life has intimate associations with it; the seamstress, and Mr. Vetch the seedy gentleman-fiddler in a low theatre (clearly derived from the impression made on James by Frederick Dorrit, as the little seamstress's selfless goodness is from Amy Dorrit); while Millicent Henning is a ludicrous imitation of Fanny Dorrit, for whom James expressed his unqualified admiration. Much more of the kind could be adduced, but is surely unnecessary.[1]

I am, sir,

Very sincerely yours,

F. R. LEAVIS

[1] Dr. Leavis ended a second letter on this theme with: "Since Mr. Putt mentions *The Bostonians*, let me put my valuation of *The Princess Casamassima* in this way: by the standard the American novel holds before us, *The Princess Casamassima* is a miserable failure."

63. Professor Roy Fuller on Shelley
To *The Times Literary Supplement*: May 21, 1971

Sir, – I should like to call Roy Fuller's attention to this sentence: "If Shelley had been born a hundred years later, the twentieth century would have seen a Newton of Chemistry." It comes from *Science and the Modern World* (p. 118), given by A. N. Whitehead as Lowell Lectures in 1925 and published in England in 1926 by the Cambridge University Press. I had (and have) a great respect for Whitehead, but remember thinking at the time how much more impressive the chapter called "The Romantic Reaction" would have been if he had not, in spite of having read the poets and realized their relevance to his theme, been so uncritically naive in regard to poetry. I am forced to say that the occupant of the Chair of Poetry at Oxford, whose non-literary distinction is hardly comparable to that of the collaborator in *Principia Mathematica*, seems to me to be, in relation to the subject he professes (May 14) no less naive.[1] By his own testimony, the account I wrote thirty-five years ago had been found convincing and decisive, and he himself (though "slightly uneasy") had not perceived how unjust to Shelley it was until he read Mr. King-Hele's refutation: "it was not until 1960", he says, "when Desmond King-Hele published his book, *Shelley: His Thought and Work,* that the rights of the matter were established".

Assuming the satisfying finality of the refutation, he says: "For, of course, the fundamental objection which Dr. Leavis is making to Shelley is his untruth to nature." That is to misrepresent, along with the explicit "objection" my critique develops, the immediate point I emphasize in relation to the given stanza of the ode. I have never doubted that Shelley had a remarkable intelligence, or that he used it to acquire a great deal of varied knowledge, some of it of the scientific kind that impressed Whitehead. My criticism in the passage that Mr. Fuller quotes from *Revaluation* regards the way in which Shelley uses language in poetry – a use that suggests that the profound Shelleyan bent was the

---

[1] Dr. Leavis is replying to Roy Fuller's Oxford Lecture "The Osmotic Sap". The main point is that the *Ode to the West Wind* was defended by some meteorologists who claimed that it gave a scientifically accurate picture of certain meteorological phenomena. But since the meteorologists were unable to agree on which meteorological phenomena Shelley was describing with such scientific accuracy, and plaints of defamation were even heard in the course of the dispute, the case is not closed. See "The Meteorology of Shelley's Ode" by F. H. Ludlam in the *TLS* for September 1, 1972, and the correspondence about it the following weeks.

antithesis of the scientist's. Summing up the account of the poet and the writing of poetry he gives in his "Defence of Poetry", I report (*Revaluation*, p. 210): "The effect of Shelley's eloquence is to hand poetry over to a sensibility that has no more dealings with intelligence than it can help." The effect of the scientific support Mr. King-Hele brings Shelley hardly tends to the demolition of this verdict. One needn't question the scientific accuracy of the detailed points with which he defends the stanza, in order to reflect that imagery which has to be explained in this way does not owe the persuasiveness it has had, and can still have, for lovers of Shelley to the kind of felicity the meteorological specialist elucidates here. The reader who finds "shook from the tangled boughs of Heaven and Ocean" potent and right (as he may go on doing after accepting Mr. King-Hele's defence) is not enjoying delicately precise and felicitous observation, but paying implicit tribute to the Shelleyan hypnoidal power, which precludes the kind of actively intelligent attention Mr. King-Hele's defence required of him — and required of Mr. Fuller.

Mr. Fuller, in fact, goes on to admit the unanswerableness of the case I put. He quotes this passage of mine which, he says, "anatomizes the poetry's main deficiency":

> in. . .a general tendency of the images to forget the status of metaphor or simile that introduced them and to assume an autonomy and a right to propagate, so that we lose in confused generalities and perspectives the perception or thought that was the ostensible *raison d'être* of imagery, we have a recognized essential trait of Shelley's: his weak grasp of the actual.

He comments: "Despite the disappearance of the crutch for the argument, the passage from the West Wind Ode, the justice of this must be admitted." The weak grasp, the slack use of language, is apparent in Shelley's rimes; a weakness, or slackness, exemplified in the "shed" that Mr. King-Hele (as adduced by Mr. Fuller) twice — from different poems — explains as felicity.

In my critique I make it plain that my "fundamental objection" goes further and deeper. It is not his "untruth to nature"; it is that the emotional luxury he invites others to share involves and propagates a self-indulgence that feels itself noble but is blindly and dangerously egocentric. "Shelley's characteristic pathos is self-regarding, directed upon an idealized self" and "for all his altruistic fervours and his fancied capacity for projecting his sympathies, Shelley is habitually his own hero" — the West Wind Ode being in question, one can point in

143

exemplification to this, which gives the nature of the whole emotional élan:

> *I fall upon the thorns of life! I bleed!*
> *A heavy weight of hours has chained and bowed*
> *One too like thee: tameless, and swift, and proud.*

"Adonais" is a triumph of intoxicated and intoxicating narcissism, the more strikingly so for offering to be a tribute of impassioned admiration for the greater dead poet, Keats.

I am, sir,

Very sincerely yours,

F. R. LEAVIS

64. The "Great Debate" about Joining Europe
To *The Times*: November 2, 1971

Sir, – The admirable letter you print (October 28) from Professor
R. S. Scorer will get no attention from either side in the "great debate." He nevertheless has an advantage over those who for my kind
of reason cannot share the sanguine attitude of *The Times* to the
prospect of "entering Europe". He concludes: "Indiscriminate
economic growth is regarded as the means without which we cannot
solve our problems. It is in danger of becoming an end in more than
one sense."

This, pollution being the issue, is obvious, unanswerable and ignored. Yet to insist on the menace of pollution won't be regarded as
just gratuitous and meaningless, even though the industrialist, economist and politician debaters, and primers of debate, decline to spoil
the effective simplicity of their criteria by recognizing such compli-
cations. But when we others, while applauding Professor Scorer, point
out that, pollution apart, to make economic growth an end in itself
is self-defeating and leads to disaster, we know that we shall not get
even from you the recognition that a serious consideration has been
raised. At any rate, we have found no reason in *The Times* for concluding otherwise.

You show yourself prepared to take cognizance of political and
constitutional doubts, and of politico-sentimental misgivings regarding
"national identity", but not of the fact that, in a civilization in which
economic growth is universally treated as an end in itself – the
supreme end, and nothing matters that can't be weighed, statistically
handled, and, if necessary, priced, any national identity worth preserving is rapidly disappearing – a process that "entering Europe"
will beyond question accelerate. No one suggests that Europe is going
to generate in compensation any kind of "identity" that the United
States hasn't. The whole campaign confirms the established habit of
accepting as sufficient criteria of human wellbeing the implications of
the assurance I have read in (I think) your pages – offered by the
advertisers as argument enough: "Joining Europe means more jobs in
Britain."

The advertising expert has judged well: this is the appropriate
appeal – to such an extent already has the reductivism represented
by such a formula triumphed. Yet your columns offer us every day
the evidence that the civilization that dooms the masses to "jobs"

with no human meaning but the pay they bring, "jobs" made sufferable only by the prospect of leisure, is precarious, sick, and far advanced on a path to death. The leisure ("culture") of such a people is provided for by commercial interests into whose calculations nothing enters but the profit-motive, or by organizations whose standards have been in essence commercially determined, and, in the process, that widespread creativity which maintains a living culture and with it the significance necessary to human life has been destroyed.

Professor Scorer, though pessimistic, can have hopes that the menace he points to will compel attention. We others know that *our* cause, though not less vital, is more desperate. But it would still encourage us if we could see, now and then, some recognition that it exists, and matters, in a paper that addresses itself to the educated — a paper of the standing of *The Times*.

I am, sir,

Very sincerely yours,

F. R. LEAVIS

65. Cambridge "English": Historical Notes and Ironies

To *The Times Literary Supplement*: March 3, 1972

Sir, – My name occurs repeatedly in your discussion (February 25) of "The State of English" at Cambridge, and in such a manner as calls for some corrective comment from me; otherwise the fallacious implication, unchallenged, would be helped on its way to becoming history, accepted and established. Not all of the references to myself are meant to be adverse; for instance, I can hardly complain of this:

> "Leavis stood for a clear idea of what Cambridge English was", one don said to me nostalgically, "he really was the only one who had a profound understanding of that tradition".

A "tradition", of course, is not necessarily a "consensus". I bring in this last word because it is used by Raymond Williams who, from your article, would appear to be a major, effectively Marxising centre of influence in the present-day Faculty. He is quoted as saying: "The consensus on which the English Faculty did its best work ended about the time of Leavis's retirement and a new consensus has yet to be worked out." Actually, so little did I, in my sense of what Cambridge English *should* be, represent a consensus, that Mr. Williams's implication exemplifies what is, for me, the most familiar of life's ironies: I was, in my academic career (if that is the word), made to feel irretrievably an outlaw, and I remained to the end conscious of being looked on by those in power as a deplorable influence – in the way registered and endorsed by the King Edward VII ex-Professor in his memoirs (where he refers to the nuisance of the "Leavisites"). Yet the article, when – as it does a number of times – it mentions my retirement, imputes to it in Mr Williams's spirit a decisive historical significance.

Since the *démenti* I have just offered was long ago neutralized as "persecution-mania", let me briefly rehearse the relevant facts. At my superannuation I was indeed a University Reader: I had been advanced to that status in my sixty-fifth year. As for my previous official standing, I was appointed as Assistant Lecturer in my early forties and a full University Lecturer in my fifties. The financial consequences for my retired years, as well as for my previous life, of such an academic career constitute, in the nature of things, a fact that I and my wife (who also – though with even less recognition – devoted a life's service to Cambridge English) can hardly regard as negligible.

These data, Sir, are surely very relevant to your inquiry. I can enforce this point by stating that, though in my sixtieth year I was admitted to the Faculty Board, I have never at any time had any say in Faculty appointments – and my wife has suffered complete exclusion.

The relevance is a matter of the obvious truth that, to committees offering to discuss "Tripos reform", I have put in this way: "What is the use of our discussing Tripos reform when we know that serious discussion of the most important head, the quality of the teaching and examining personnel, is prohibited?" That kind of question itself, of course, constituted a Leavisite nuisance. I will only permit myself to say further with regard to this order of consideration that anyone who supposes there to be more possibility now than in earlier days of the kind of person getting into the Faculty who would fight intelligently and effectively, or even resolutely, for – to use Mr Williams's word – a redeeming kind of "consensus", exhibits an extreme lack of realism.

As for the assumptions involved in the identifying of me with "Practical Criticism", my first comment is that the formula isn't mine, and, as hundreds of old pupils will testify, I have been known for my insistence, when having to use it, that "Practical criticism is criticism in practice". My own published criticism, which bears a close relation to my work with undergraduates, testifies, I think, that I have never thought of the critical discipline as something to be identified with the analysis of patches, short pieces, and extracts that can be contained on a page or an examination paper. I have always insisted that if an English School isn't committed to the defence and vindication of literary study as representing a distinctive discipline of intelligence, it has no serious claim to exist, and that the discipline in question is the critical, seriously conceived and practised. In defaulting, it fails the other disciplines in relation to which it properly has its existence at the university.

But "discipline", to judge by your article, is a word that has acquired a peculiar meaning in the present "State of Cambridge English" – and of the *TLS* too. Your contributor refers to George Steiner as representing a "general tendency. . . towards the inter-disciplinary approach". Vital relations *between* the different disciplines are indeed highly to be desired. But what Dr. Steiner represents, it seems to me, is the kind of intellectuality behind which there is no discipline of any kind. And that, I gather from the article, as from other evidence, is the kind of intellectuality that the Cambridge English School, though it excludes Dr. Steiner, is going more and more to aim at producing. It adjusts itself so to our new civilization.

I must add in conclusion that the significance your representative attributes to L. C. Knights's change into an anti-*Scrutiny* attitude is illusory: after the early days his connexion with *Scrutiny* was not merely negligible but deprecatory and the effective editing and the major contributions, like the actual work, were carried out by my wife and myself.

I am, sir,
Very sincerely yours,
F. R. LEAVIS

66. Literature and Society
To *The Spectator*: November 4, 1972

Sir, — The practice of calling attention to my insignificance by dragging in my name gratuitously is one with which readers of reviews are familiar: there are two instances in your issue for October 28. One of them, that in a review by Richard Luckett of a book by Laurence Lerner, damages only the reviewer and (possibly) the author. I have inserted the 'possibly' to allow for the loose unspecificity of the insinuated charge: "the Leavisite confusion between the health of a literature and the health of a society". It is at any rate possible that the author himself, even if he shares your reviewer's reliance on the applause of an anti-Leavisite solidarity, sees that to pooh-pooh crudely the belief in an essential relation between the health of a literature and the health of a society is to commit oneself to incoherence and dilettantism and deny that literature really matters.

If I let the other instance pass I might be taken to have given tacit endorsement to viciously false implications. In reviewing H. A. Mason's *To Homer Through Pope* Christopher Gill writes: "At such moments we hear only too clearly the sound of the lectures from which the book was adapted; and, behind Mason's orotund tones, we hear another flat but penetrating voice, that of F. R. Leavis". Your reviewer hears what he hears, but I assure him that, while I know actually nothing about Mr Mason's lectures, I do know, from such numbers as I have seen of the *Cambridge Quarterly*, of which I have noticed that he is editor-in-chief, that the suggestion of affinities in critical position, intention and bent between his criticism, or that of which he approves, and mine, is ludicrously wide of the mark. It has been reliably and repeatedly reported to me that the university teachers behind whose instruction Mr Mason's voice is to be heard deplore and dismiss, along with my criticism in general, all that I have written about Pope.

I have not written on Pope's Homer.

I am, sir,

Very sincerely yours,

F. R. LEAVIS

67. *The Human World*
To *The Listener*: January 18, 1973

Sir, — My attention has been called to the article on *The Human World* by P. N. Furbank in the *Listener* for 4 January. It contains misconceptions that ought not to become current. I was not personally involved in any way in the genesis of the quarterly, I have no part in its direction, and it is surprising to me that Mr Furbank should be able to see in its contents a 'uniformity' that he explains as the result of an editorial policy of propagating my views.

I find myself (expecting to do so) disagreeing with a good many things that it publishes. I deplored, for instance, G. E. M. Anscombe's article in No 7: 'Contraception and Chastity'. More generally, I am surprised at the suggestion that there is an affinity between me and Wittgenstein, or any concurrence of 'influence', and nothing I have read in *The Human World* seems to me to lend plausibility to such ideas. The editors themselves are aware that I lack intellectual sympathy with Wittgenstein.[1] Real intellectual and cultural life entails the creative play of differences, some of which may find expression as strong disagreements. Certainly the collaboration represented by a cultural organ ought not to be the kind of consensus that Mr Furbank describes. The editors of *The Human World* obviously know that too.

I am, sir,

Very sincerely yours,

F. R. LEAVIS

[1] See Dr. Leavis's "Memories of Wittgenstein" in *The Human World*, No. 10, February, 1973.

INDEX

INDEX

INDEX

INDEX

Nor Shall My Sword, 13, 16, 132n., 135n., 136n.

Observer, The, 78, 83
O'Connor, Maureen, 100-1
'Ode to the West Wind', 142n., 143
Old Curiosity Shop, The, 96
Old Pretender, 107
Open university, 128
Oresteia, 61, 63
Organic community, the, 15, 100-1, 137
'Orthodoxy of Enlightenment, The', 84n.
Orwell, George, 73, 118n.
Osborne (in *Journey's End*), 123
'Osmotic Sap, The', 142
Othello, 40-1
Othello, 12, 40-1
'Outsider, The', 111n.
Overseas Readers, 37
'Owl and the Nightingale, The', 116
Oxford, 11, 103, 116, 118, 142
Oxford Chair of Poetry, 53
Oxford History of English Literature, 106
Oxford Review, 119

'Palace of Art, The', 123
Paradise Lost, 33, 66, 67, 68
'Paradise Lost' and Its Critics, 33
Parkes, H.B., 113
Parody, 31, 91-3
Peter, John, 68
Ph.D. Research, 80, 103-4
Pierce, Grace, 52
Pisan Cantos, The, 79, 139
Pittock, Malcolm, 133
Plato, 48, 49
Plurality of critical centres, 57
Poetic drama, 40-1

'Poetic Renascence, The', 44
Poetics, The, 76
Poetry Direct and Oblique, 54
Pollution, 145
Pope, 92, 121, 150
Portrait of a Lady, The, 35, 140
Pound, Ezra, 12n., 25, 66, 79, 81-2, 83, 139
Powys, T.F., 98
Practical criticism, 46-7, 75-6, 148
Preface to Shakespeare, 121-2
Prentice-Hall, 39n.
Price, Christopher, 137
Price, R.G.G., 107
Priestley, J.B., 10, 21n., 56-7
Princess Casamassima, The, 12, 106-7, 140-1
Principia Mathematica, 142
Pritchett, V.S., 12, 12n., 43
Propagandist for criticism, 11
Pryce-Jones, Alan, 38
Puddn'head Wilson, 52
Putt, R. Gorley, 140-1

'Questions of Degree', 109
Quiller-Couch, A., 75

Raleigh, W., 66-8
Raymond, John, 38
Reardon, B.M.G., 94
Reeves, James, 56
Rejected Addresses, 91
Religious instruction, 117
Renaissance, The, 116
'Research in English', 105n.
Revaluation, 53, 88, 90n., 142-4
Richards, I.A., 26, 46
Richmond Lecture, 101
Ricks, Christopher, 14, 114
Robbins Report, 110, 130
Robeson, Paul, 40

158

INDEX

INDEX

Trilling, Lionel, 107
Troilus and Cressida, 85
Troilus and Criseyde, 85
Trollope, 43
Turnell, Martin, 84
Tuve, Rosemond, 11, 13, 66-8
Twain, Mark, 52
Twentieth Century Views Series, 39n.
Two Cultures? 101

Ulysses (Joyce), 18, 97-9
University of the Air, 111
Uses of Literacy, The, 58

Verse Chronicle, 24
Vetch, Mr, 141

Wagner, Robert, 48
Wain, John, 69-70
Waldock, A.J.A., 33, 68
Walton, Geoffrey, 47
Warton lectures, 53
Watson, Patricia M., 133
'We are the End', 24

Welfare State, The, 51
Wellek, René, 48
Wells, H.G., 107
West, Rebecca, 35
Wheelwright's Shop, The, 100
Whitehead, A.N., 142
Willey, Basil, 135, 147
Williams, Charles, 67
Williams, Raymond, 147-8
Wilson, Harold, 128
Winters, Yvor, 124
Wittgenstein, 151
Wodehouse, P.G., 118
Women in Love, 60-3, 65, 84, 134
Woolwich, Bishop of, 85n.
Woolworths, 99
Wordsworth, 91
Working-class culture, 14, 15, 58

Yeats, W.B., 31, 83
York University, 115, 137
Young Goodman Brown, 39

Zuleika Dobson, 107